# The Compliance Busi. its Customers

I0011257

# The Compliance Business and its Customers

## Gaining Competitive Advantage by Controlling Your Customers

**Edward Kasabov**

*Associate Professor, University of Exeter Business School, Exeter, United Kingdom*

and

**Alex Warlow**

*Director, Noridol Ltd*

palgrave
macmillan

© Edward Kasabov & Alex Warlow 2012

All rights reserved. No reproduction, copy or transmission of this
publication may be made without written permission.

No portion of this publication may be reproduced, copied or transmitted
save with written permission or in accordance with the provisions of the
Copyright, Designs and Patents Act 1988, or under the terms of any licence
permitting limited copying issued by the Copyright Licensing Agency,
Saffron House, 6–10 Kirby Street, London EC1N 8TS.

Any person who does any unauthorized act in relation to this publication
may be liable to criminal prosecution and civil claims for damages.

The authors have asserted their rights to be identified as the authors of this
work in accordance with the Copyright, Designs and Patents Act 1988.

First published 2012 by
PALGRAVE MACMILLAN

Palgrave Macmillan in the UK is an imprint of Macmillan Publishers Limited,
registered in England, company number 785998, of Houndmills, Basingstoke,
Hampshire RG21 6XS.

Palgrave Macmillan in the US is a division of St Martin's Press LLC,
175 Fifth Avenue, New York, NY 10010.

Palgrave Macmillan is the global academic imprint of the above companies
and has companies and representatives throughout the world.

Palgrave® and Macmillan® are registered trademarks in the United States,
the United Kingdom, Europe and other countries.

ISBN 978-1-349-32934-2        ISBN 978-1-137-27115-0 (eBook)
DOI 10.1057/9781137271150

This book is printed on paper suitable for recycling and made from fully
managed and sustained forest sources. Logging, pulping and manufacturing
processes are expected to conform to the environmental regulations of the
country of origin.

A catalogue record for this book is available from the British Library.

A catalog record for this book is available from the Library of Congress.

10  9  8  7  6  5  4  3  2  1
21 20 19 18 17 16 15 14 13 12

# Contents

# List of Tables, Figures and Exhibit

## Tables

## Figures

## Exhibit

# List of Cases in Point

# Preface

> Throughout this book, readers will find lists of bullet points in boxes at the start and end of sections and chapters. These points summarise key arguments which are of use for practitioners, managers, academics and students.
>
> o *This book seeks to describe and make sense of significant changes in thinking which have taken place in marketing practice and business strategy in the last 20 years which we term 'customer compliance' and which have profited from the introduction of new technologies such as the Internet.*
> o *In this book we also examine management and marketing innovations designed and implemented by practitioners across sectors, linking them to marketing and strategy theory and extant research*
> o *Readers should develop a clearer understanding of competitiveness through the application of modern technology.*

Marketing as an academic study has inherited the thinking, methodologies and communication of the academic disciplines which have informed thinking in the area, including the natural sciences, mathematics, statistics, psychology and sociology. However, our discipline also draws heavily from ideas and images which are prominent in the humanities and arts. The debate whether marketing is an art or science continues to this day; however, much of its growth and maturation in the twentieth century has been marked by attempts to apply and use approaches which appeared more 'scientific', and therefore reputable and legitimate. The resulting ideas, theories and the accepted ways of researching these ideas have become the norm in the marketing discipline, largely mimicking approaches taken in the natural sciences. These ideas have found their way into textbooks and have been presented to generations of students as objective, immutable facts.

The introduction and growing use of computers in the last 20 years, the ability to link computers, as well as more recent developments in technology and communications have assisted marketing practitioners in designing, applying and refining highly innovative strategies and techniques to manage their customers and business partners, with little or no reference to the traditional marketing approaches. While new technologies have supported the application of such novel marketing approaches, it is the ingenuity and ideas of marketing practitioners that have broken path-dependent norms to such an extent that new businesses have grown to replace traditional businesses across sectors.

One-to-one marketing, predicated on amassing large amounts of data about individuals along with automated marketing, made possible by the application of novel technological solutions, has replaced or questioned the utility of traditional segmentation, mass advertising and the over-emphasis on branding. Traditional value chains have collapsed under the weight of such developments. Most of the new initiatives designed and implemented by innovative marketing practitioners have risen through trial and error – a process which is cheaper, quicker and more effortless thanks to the development of technology solutions, particularly online and call-centre solutions enabled by innovative back-office software. Trialling new ideas and rapidly evolving novel strategies can be done quickly, even automatically and in real time, making much traditional market and marketing research obsolete.

Current marketing theories cannot adequately describe and accurately explain some of the innovations introduced by marketing practitioners referred to here and analysed in the remainder of this book. Such short-comings make it increasingly difficult to teach marketing as a discipline in the Internet age, in spite of the proliferation of courses focusing on specific techniques such as email marketing or data mining. What we feel is missing is an overarching marketing theory which will allow marketing theorists to teach the next generation of marketing managers by revealing to them significant marketing problems and the current approaches to solving them.

This book sheds light on, and makes sense of, some technology-enabled innovations introduced by marketing practitioners which should stimulate thinking about what it is that some businesses do so well and why they have proved successful against their more traditional rivals. Our discussion questions current marketing frameworks and thoughts, in light of the practitioner innovations discussed here. We aim not only to help close the gap between practitioners' actions and academics' research but also provide opportunities for managers to benchmark themselves against the innovative business practices analysed in the book. The lesson for marketers, we would like to believe, is that marketing practice is not fixed and immutable – it is rapidly changing, inventive and may have something valuable to offer social thinking more generally.

The marketing practitioners, their businesses and the practices which they have invented that we describe here may appear to be too disparate and sharing little in common. They span across sectors and industries. Some are relatively new ventures, whereas others are traditional companies which have reinvented themselves. What unites them is the source of their competitive success – their ability to recognise, and eagerness to embrace, the advantages offered by rapidly developing technologies. Customer compliance is what unites these marketing practitioners, their businesses and the practices that they have introduced and which, we argue, are here to stay. Customer compliance, as practiced by these businesses, has come to question some long-held assumptions in marketing practice and theory, most notably the concept of customer centricity. The alternative, customer compliance approach to managing relations with customers, business partners and other stakeholders lowers costs of operation, contributes to business profitability and competitive advantage, and does not hurt customer satisfaction.

One example of a customer compliance business discussed by us is the low-cost airline Ryanair. Despite considerable criticism, on the part of the press, public authorities and even academics, of its treatment of customers, the company has been growing by attracting increasing numbers of customers while successfully retaining many of its current clients. If their customer management practices are as bad as some commentators claim, why is this company so successful? The ability of customer compliance businesses such as Ryanair to attract and keep customers and to grow their sectors, by taking market share from traditional competitors in these markets, needs to be understood. Hence, we asked ourselves the following question long before the very idea for writing this book: If such customer compliance businesses treat their customers so badly, why are they growing and increasing their profitability, while the traditional competitors of such companies, such as the legacy airlines, continue to lose market share?

In an attempt to explain how and why innovative marketing practitioners have effectively made their customers 'compliant' with their company requirements, while offering them significant enough benefits to retain their business, we also present some solutions to problems in sustaining competitive advantage in this age of hyper-competition and unpredictable company fortunes. Hence, the title of this book: 'The Compliance Business and its Customers: How to achieve sustained success using new technologies' as a useful label to describe the wide range of new and exciting marketing practices and businesses which have embraced technology and have learnt to use it to innovate marketing thinking by breaking path dependent norms and competing in novel ways.

---

## Summary for managers:

o *Innovative marketing strategies have rapidly evolved, enabled by developments in information and communication technology in the last 20 years.*
o *Developments have affected all sectors in developed economies. In certain sectors they have challenged the supremacy of incumbent businesses.*
o *The common theme which best describes these practices is 'customer compliance' whereby companies adopting 'compliance' practices make their customers, business partners and other stakeholders comply with their systems, benefiting those involved.*
o *'Customer compliance' is about ignoring or even excluding complainers and costly dissatisfied customers.*
o *In return for complying with company expectations, systems and procedures, 'good' customers are rewarded with lower prices and, in many cases, good or adequate service.*
o *Although 'customer compliance' may appear counter-intuitive and disadvantaging companies practicing it, many 'customer compliance' businesses appear to have competitive advantage, displacing incumbents and attracting customers despite the negative publicity which they attract.*

# Introduction

**Key questions in this chapter:**

o *How have IT and modern communications affected your business?*
o *Has technology made you more competitive or less?*
o *Have your competitors made better use of technology?*
o *Have modern technologies made you redesign your company strategy, marketing, service recovery and market research?*
o *Do you consider your company to be customer centric, or do you practise something else, for instance controlling your customers in some way?*

In the last 20 years, businesses taking advantage of market deregulation and novel call centre, Intranet and Internet technologies have broken traditional marketing norms and customer management practices. These businesses offer good customer service at substantially lower prices. In spite of anecdotal evidence in the press of the high level of customer complaints against these businesses, their success is evidenced by their ability to take market share from existing businesses and grow new profitable markets.

Examples of what we refer to in this book as 'customer compliance' businesses are found across sectors, including telecommunications (NTL), TV and broadband supply (BT, Virgin/NTL), low-cost air travel (Ryanair, easyJet), banking (Egg), insurance and financial services (Directline, E-sure), travel and tourism (Expedia, Holiday Extras, Booking.com), car rental (Holiday Autos), provision of goods (Amazon), online auctions (eBay) and retail (Tesco, IKEA).

Service provision and interactions with customers in terms of empowerment and what academics refer to as 'democratisation' are areas which have been extensively re-designed by these businesses. Customer compliance businesses tend to remove serial complainers from their databases and always consider the benefits to the majority of their customers rather than pandering to the demands of the relatively small number of complainers. The currently dominant discourse in marketing teaches us that marketing practitioners should seek the views of their customers, fulfil their customers' needs and demands, and listen to complainers' feedback as a form of market and marketing research. Instead, customer compliance businesses tend to concentrate on serving well and pleasing the majority of their customers, which allows them to grow their business rapidly, while ignoring complainers, who are not seen as a legitimate source of new business ideas and suggestions for service innovations.

Further innovations trialled and successfully applied by customer compliance businesses include their collaboration with what could be termed 'good customers'. They are non-complainers and economically profitable customers who are invited to use the platforms of customer compliance businesses and, in the process of doing so, contribute to the overall process of service provision. However, such customer contributions reveal one more key feature of compliance – businesses invite customers to collaborate only in areas where customer compliance businesses 'allow' them to co-produce service, thus generating a certain level of, possibly superficial, empowerment. Examples which we discuss at some length include customer recommendations and feedback as well as self-help forums, which are increasingly used by businesses to improve products and services. Our initial casual observations, backed by empirical evidence collected during four rounds of longitudinal qualitative and quantitative research involving customers and staff of such businesses in 2008–11, demonstrate that mediated interactions with 'good customers' which make heavy use of new technologies not only make customers feel empowered in some ways but also restrict their input into more fundamental aspects of service provision.

By forcing customers to 'comply' with their policies and rules of service provision, customer compliance businesses reduce the costs of operation and offer partly pre-designed customer experiences which appear to be accepted by the majority of their customers. In spite of the obvious restrictions of customer compliance practices, much misunderstood by academics, the general press and even some practitioners, it appears that a certain level of 'disciplining' and 'governing' of the behaviour of customers has proved to be key to the successful operation of these businesses. Hence the term 'compliance' was born. The term does not necessarily imply that customers are being forced to behave in a certain manner against their will but that they tend to be rewarded with a high level of service at low price if they are willing to comply with pre-set company systems and processes of interactions.

This book aims to present a holistic account of the nature and consequences of these businesses, by identifying and making sense of some more important aspects of the operation of customer compliance businesses and the marketing practitioner innovations which make these compliance businesses successful. Although the application of new technology in marketing and its effect on database marketing, CRM, e-marketing, digital marketing and e-commerce are not new, and even though much has been written about each of these developments and concepts, customer compliance businesses and the type of marketing and customer management practices that they have designed and implemented are truly revolutionary and hence deserve a proper analysis. They offer opportunities for benchmarking in times of recession, and for understanding the basis of sustained competitive advantage in an age which provides few options for lasting success.

In this book – aimed primarily at a practitioner audience but also applicable to students of service marketing, relationship marketing, e-marketing, and marketing strategy, among others – we critically revisit key concepts in services marketing, marketing strategy and marketing management, such as customer centricity, service provision, service failure and recovery. Although the more prominent theoretical-academic approaches to tackling these issues are presented, our discussion does not aim to be overly theoretical but focuses on the provision of empirical illustrations of current practice, in order to demonstrate the novelty of some practitioners' thinking and experimentations.

Chapter 1 defines the parameters of customer compliance and customer compliance businesses by explaining what is meant by terms used throughout the book, such as 'customer compliance', 'customer compliance management' and 'customer compliance businesses'. It also provides an initial overview of the types of compliance businesses which we consider for the remainder of the discussion.

In Chapter 2 we trace the origins of customer compliance, searching for clues in recent developments and economic changes in the landscape across industries, including globalisation, deregulation, liberalisation and privatisation. The unleashing of these forces has coincided with a period of rapid introduction of earlier mentioned communications and data storage technologies. Due attention is paid to the rise of e-commerce, by carefully delineating the boundary between customer compliance businesses and other businesses using e-commerce.

Building upon the coverage and assessment of technology developments, Chapter 3 demonstrates the innovative applications of technology by customer compliance businesses. Here we cover the opportunities that customer compliance businesses have detected and exploited in areas of automated computerised systems, data management and database marketing.

Being the first of four 'core' chapters which investigate different aspects of technology-enabled marketing innovations which underlie the success of customer compliance businesses, Chapter 4 introduces in detail major innovations which set customer compliance businesses apart from their rivals. The path-breaking thinking characteristic of customer compliance businesses takes various expressions, each of them deserving a separate treatment and each of them analysed against the background of normative thinking in marketing about precepts of service provision. For instance, the way in which these businesses organise their service provision generally, and more specifically towards 'difficult' customers, is vital to cost reduction and 'customer education'. Separate sections explore the service recovery and complaint management practices of these businesses, the unique role that front-line personnel play in compliance implementation, and the approach that these businesses adopt towards customer empowerment, which sets them apart from other businesses.

Following the coverage of innovations in service provision, we describe and assess innovations introduced in areas of market and marketing research in Chapter 5. Market and marketing research have been substantially altered as part of the model of operation of innovative businesses. Opening with a brief overview of nature of traditional research, we proceed with a detailed analysis of the manner in which conventional models, methods and approaches to research in marketing have been replaced by trial and error methods which, once again, depend on and embrace a mix of varied new technologies. New research practices benefit from the low cost of website-based experimentation, real-time research and online methods of direct interactions with customers.

A question which has preoccupied practitioners and academics for some time is how companies attain and sustain their competitive advantage. In Chapter 6, we bring together key aspects of operations and the innovations designed and carried out by the customer compliance businesses in order to identify the ingredients of their new business model which has helped this set of entrepreneurial companies to dominate the sectors in which they compete. The sources, nature and consequences of this new business model are highlighted. Partly because there exists no consensus regarding the definition, nature, structure and evolution of business models, the notion of a customer compliance business model holds some promise as a unifying unit of analysis that can facilitate not only practice – through benchmarking – but also theory development.

Much has been written about the companies studied by us here. In academic studies, practitioner reports and, especially, the general press, instances of negative and sometimes tendentious accounts are easily uncovered. We assess such coverage, in Chapter 7, as part of our attempt to understand and conceptualise the reaction of various constituencies to the innovations of these businesses. Misunderstanding the nature and benefits of customer compliance seems to account for such negative coverage. It is particularly imperative to describe and explain such misunderstanding on the part of some academics and practitioners and also to offer an alternative thesis of customer compliance and its effects on customers, business partners, sectors and society as a whole. Most important, in that respect, has been the reaction of consumers, and it is here that we draw upon our empirical research in order to demonstrate that in spite of stories of widespread consumer apathy and dissatisfaction with customer compliance businesses, consumers demonstrate remarkable loyalty and keep on voting with their wallets.

No account of new business thinking would be complete without a glimpse into the future and a tentative prediction about trends and directions of service provision and customer compliance. We grappled with questions in Chapter 8, where the discussion of some more pressing issues continues with an analysis of the influence of customer compliance businesses on competition and its likely future effect. An assessment is on offer of whether the business model described throughout the book is likely to be sustained and if it can be replicated across a wider range of industries and by a number of different types of organisations, including the public and third sectors. Although complex business ethics issues which arise from the introduction of such marketing innovations are outside the immediate interest of this book, A select few areas of moral and ethical import are also briefly addressed in Chapter 8, in an attempt to provide some pointers about rights, obligations, responsibility and controls.

---

### *Chapter summary for managers:*

o *Correctly identifying customer needs, profitable customer segments and types of customers are key to marketing and business success.*

o *It may be more advantageous to ignore or even remove (exclude) serial complainers, concentrating instead on customers who are profitable – defined as 'good customers'.*

o *Designing and applying standardised procedures and inflexible systems can cut costs of service provision by introducing clear transparent rules to which all customers are expected to adhere.*

o *Using modern technology allows quick, cheap alteration of such procedures and systems, in real time and when required.*

o *Staff who are knowledgeable of such standardised procedures and inflexible systems know how to react to customer complaints. Customer compliance tends to empower front-line, help-line and customer service staff.*

---

# 1 Defining and Understanding Customer Compliance

### Key questions in this chapter:

o *Have you defined and studied your marketing activities and company strategy in terms of Customer Relationship Management and customer centricity?*

o *Do you invest considerable resources to try and meet the needs of vocal dissatisfied customers and serial complainers?*

o *Do you use knowledge that you possess about your customers to control them, channel their behaviour and make them compliant in some way by making them follow pre-designed and inflexible systems and rules of interaction with your company staff?*

o *Do you think that your customers benefit from being made compliant – for instance, through lower price, good or adequate service?*

o *If competitors take market share from you, have you analysed their strategy in terms of their interactions with customers?*

o *Have you or any of your staff been on training courses to fully understand the possibilities of using new technologies to redesign interactions with customers and your business partners?*

## 1.1 How practitioners and academics understand compliance

'Compliance' as a concept is not new in business practice. In the UK context, references to 'customer compliance' tend to be found in public sector analyses of benefit fraud squads in charge of 'verifying' the employment status of individuals who have signed up with JobCentres. More generally, practitioner and academic studies apply the term 'compliance' to describe the actions that relevant authorities take in order to deal with fraud allegations. For example, cases of alleged benefit fraud are investigated by 'customer compliance' officers who are also in charge of benefit reviews and may be asked to carry out interviews with suspects.

Academia offers a greater number and variety of approaches towards the analysis of 'compliance', even if most references to the term are uncovered in contexts very different from the one that is immediately relevant to our discussion – marketing. Typically the term appears to denote regulatory or legal compliance, sharing an obvious commonality with the dominant prac-titioner discourse described above. Examples of this thesis are found not only in legal studies but also in applied economics, and more specifically in studies on regulatory compliance in banking and finance,[1] on trust in authorities who exact compliance,[2] and on employers' respecting expecta-tions and state regulations concerning various aspects of taxation, environ-mental, and labour law, such as conditions of employment, minimum wage,[3] occupational safety,[4] and pollution.[5]

Political science and international relations research has tackled slightly different expressions of compliance, in terms of observance and fulfilment of national taxation system expectations and requirements.[6] Exacting compli-ance of this type requires the design and implementation of systematic and regular checks, in turn accounting for the interest of political scientists and commentators in monitoring and auditing against codified standards and expectations of individual and collective-corporate behaviour, as forms of compliance management. Whereas in most other social science disci-plines the origin, source and point of reference of compliance management is the state, in political science the state itself is also treated as answerable to supra-national institutions, their regulations[7] and the expectations arising from state membership (Simmons 2010) – thus giving birth to notions of national-level compliance.

The review of relevant work across the social sciences is not meant to be exhaustive but representative; for, in spite of the variety of contexts and types of cases and issues discussed by authors, these analyses share a common view of compliance as obedience and submission to clearly stipulated regulations which are defined and exacted by, or on behalf of, an internal or external authority. In the more general area of management studies, of which mar-keting is a member, the treatment of compliance is not dissimilar to what we have already described. Compliance refers to adherence, typically on the part of a business, to a set of rules which are morally and ethically agreed upon by society and which are codified and enforced by the higher authority of the state, an arm of the state, or an institution sanctioned to oversee and enforce adherence to these standards. There is a strong inclination, in management research, to embed descriptions and evaluations of compliance in a broader understanding of the ethical and moral dimensions of company behaviour,[8] rather than limit the treatment to coverage of regulatory and legal issues, as is frequently done in economic research. The tendency to tie together moral-ethical and legal aspects of compliance is particularly common in human resource management studies, while analyses of compliance in marketing are few, of recent origin, and not particularly prominent in this discipline. The little that marketing academics have written and commented upon with respect to this important issue has been in the area of marketing systems, channel management,[9] and more specifically about managing channel con-flict by enforcing compliance. Three additional areas where the term has been entertained to some extent are consumer behaviour, social marketing[10] and medical marketing[11] with its specialist but cross-disciplinary *Journal of*

*Health Care Compliance*, much due to the ethical and legal ramifications of non-compliance with drug and research regulatory regimes. More recently, Stremersch and Van Dyck[12] have provided an example of compliance in marketing, with respect to marketing life science products. They consider differences between technology-enabled and CRM-enabled compliance programmes, and discuss the ways in which life science companies consider compliance programmes. Apart from these studies and Dellande's[13] research into practices of forcing customers to adhere a service provider's proscription while the customer is away from the provider, marketing scholars and service marketers in particular seem to have downplayed the term. Thus, the line of work that Dellande and collaborators have recently produced is a sole example of service marketing academics' interest in, and even mention of, the concept in terms of customer commitment, adherence, and following instructions and with a view to service goal attainment, but in the context of healthcare service provision only.

## 1.2   What we mean by compliance

The conception of compliance advanced in this book is distinct from views outlined in the preceding summary review of varied literatures on the subject. Distinct is the lack of emphasis on ethical and moral aspects of submission and conformity, as part of the understanding of compliance advanced in this discussion. Although ethical ramifications of customer compliance policies of the businesses analysed by us are considered, they are not at the heart of the customer compliance model whose outlines are drawn in subsequent chapters. This predilection to analyse functional aspects of customer compliance, at the expense of critical evaluations and possibly the deconstruction of such practices, has been criticised in the past by fellow academics. However, such an approach to thinking about compliance is not coincidental; to us, customer compliance denotes principally a set of innovations in areas of customer relationship management as expressed in the manner in which businesses design and develop relations with their customers more generally and especially with customers who are perceived as 'difficult' and therefore both emotionally and economically unprofitable. Compliance, or governing the behaviour of customers and partners through restriction and disciplining, to the advantage of the customer compliance business, affects all stages of service provision and interactions with these companies but is most pronounced when service provision fails and marketing theory expects the customer compliance businesses to invest considerable resources and effort to satisfy dissatisfied customers.

Our definition of compliance may remind one of earlier concepts in marketing and especially critical marketing theory, most notably the Foucauldian notion of disciplining, which is more widely known and used in marketing than compliance[14] and which denotes the shift in modern social management from visible and physical forms of control and punishment towards the more continuous and refined application of power that rests on observing and amassing knowledge through documenting one's behaviours. With disciplining suggesting that knowledge can be effectively harnessed to channel someone's behaviour in specific ways which suit a company, the link to compliance is clear. However, compliance is also distinct and separate from disciplining, in that it is viewed as a type of control which some businesses utilise for the purposes of cost-effective service provision. Whereas disciplining may apply to any aspect of service provision and to any provider that is eager to subtly control the behaviour and even the behavioural options available to customers, compliance helps explain particular practices of controlling and channelling the behaviours which are less hidden, are typically technology-driven and are found among a relatively small set of highly successful, mainly online businesses in the past decade or so. In a direct opposition to disciplining, compliance is more visible than the type of control and social management defined and theorised by Foucault – a significant aspect of compliance which will be explained in detail in later sections. Where disciplining aims to be hidden and secretive, compliance systems and procedures are designed to be more obvious, transparent and often openly discussed by the companies practising them, in order to make customers learn to conform and behave in a way that the companies' compliance procedures require. This generally benefits customers through better service and lower price, as illustrated by the dramatic growth of compliance-practising companies such as low-cost airlines and by the ability of such businesses to attract and retain customers. Customers who do not conform are typically excluded or are persuaded to exclude themselves from service provision.

In order to turn customers into willing participants in compliance practices, businesses have learned to communicate clearly benefits of complying both to service providers and their customers. Considering that customer compliance practices may appear unusual and, in some cases, opposed to the type of relationships to which customers have traditionally become accustomed, customer compliance businesses openly explain the changes that they have introduced and what these changes mean for customers and society. Thus, 'educating' existing and potential customers as well as other internal and external constituencies has become a priority for such companies, whereby they use various marketing communications channels to inform audiences about compliance practices and to persuade current and potential customers of the benefits of compliance.

Customer compliance needs to be discussed, and defined, in the context of customer centricity and associated currently dominant marketing concepts which are related to, and derivative from, customer centricity and customer orientation, such as marketing orientation, relationship marketing and CRM. Although customer centricity and associated terms tend to be differently, and at times rather loosely, defined by academics and practitioners, they tend to describe and advocate the capacity to understand, respond to and even anticipate customer needs. By juxtaposing customer compliance and customer centricity, we do not suggest that new businesses employing the former philosophical orientation are less customer centric. Their success in taking market share from incumbents, growing or transforming industries and sectors demonstrates their ability to correctly identify current customer needs and gaps in market offers, and to please their customers more than traditional competitors that purport to practise customer centricity. Although in the process of addressing customer needs and demands, the new breed of businesses analysed here make their customers compliant to their systems and expectations, we firmly believe that customer compliance businesses are truly customer centric – a key trait which helps explain their competitive advantage over allegedly customer centric incumbents, some of which are actually more product- rather than customer centric.

---

### *Chapter summary for managers:*

o *At times, practitioners develop innovations intuitively and may not try to and conceptualise them in theoretical terms, in order to make sense of the causes of their business success. This discussion should help improve understanding of success through customer compliance.*

o *Compliance is not a new concept in the social and management sciences and elsewhere. It refers to systems used to control customers and other stakeholders.*

o *In this book, customer compliance refers to a relatively new phenomenon of strategising through controlling customers and other stakeholders for the benefit of both the businesses practising compliance and their customers who are rewarded with lower prices and good or adequate service.*

o *Customer compliance denotes a set of innovations in relating to customers which appear to provide the businesses practising them with competitive advantage.*

o *Customer compliance affects all stages and aspects of service provision, including fulfilment, customer service, complaint management, market and marketing research, and pricing.*

o *Customer compliance is technology-mediated type of marketing, achieved through algorithms and automated marketing systems.*

o *Compliance has democratised service provision.*

# 2 How Did it All Come About?

---

**Key questions in this chapter:**

o *Has the business sector in which you compete been deregulated? If so, how have you taken advantage of such deregulation?*
o *Is your business working with a long supply chain or do you use the Internet to interact directly with your customers and business partners?*
o *Do you practise one-to-one marketing?*
o *Have you automated your marketing activities in any way?*
o *Have you or any of your staff recently been on training courses in order to fully understand the business opportunities that new technology provides?*
o *If you have introduced new technology systems in your business, are they systemic and do they affect the whole of your business or have they been introduced in a piecemeal fashion to specific departments, functions and activities?*
o *Do you believe businesses should concentrate on pleasing and meeting the needs of 'good' profitable customers only or do you spend time and money to resolve requests, complaints and questions of vocal dissatisfied customers and customers who keep on calling your staff with the same query?*

---

## 2.1 Regulatory and economic sources of customer compliance

Regulated and sheltered environments found across sectors in developed economies have traditionally protected incumbents,[1] including those long-established and entrenched competitors which have been described as 'national champions'. However, regulatory protection discouraged innovation, and was marked by output, price, entry and other controls aimed at restricting destructive competition. Recent deregulation, globalisation, trade liberalisation and privatisation in transportation, utilities, financial service provision and other sectors have forced companies to revisit questions of firm boundary[2] and become more entrepreneurial and creative. The combination of rising disposable incomes (partly enabled by the above changes), technological developments such as the advent of the Internet and call centre technologies, and deregulation has re-shaped sectoral landscapes,[3] favouring the emergence and rapid growth of new businesses[4] such as online auction sites and low-cost airlines. This combined regulatory, economic and technological revolution has also invalidated conventional concepts in strategy and marketing,[5] forcing practitioners to rethink their view of marketing strategy and re-write the fundamentals of competitiveness, as will be demonstrated in this and subsequent chapters.

As noted above, in the pre-deregulation era, incumbents were protected by national governments and national regulatory regimes from the 'rigors' of competition.[6] Regulatory and, consequently, economic protection cultivated complacency, bureaucratic rigidity, and management slack. It discouraged innovative thinking, particularly with respect to strategising, marketing, and managing relations with customers. Not surprisingly, the stakes of preserving this order were high, and incumbents across sectors were among the most ardent defenders of this inherited regime – deregulation proved to be the single most significant challenge to their interests.

Examples abound of deregulation driving industry change and, more specifically, the growth of customer compliance businesses. The airline industry, among the first to be dramatically redesigned by customer compliance arrivals, was highly regulated until the early 1990s. In the US, it had been subject to extensive regulation since 1937, with the federal Civil Aeronautics Board regulating a number of aspects of interstate air transportation, including pricing and entry into the industry. Only certain airlines were allowed to serve specific routes, and the USA and other countries were eager to protect their flag carriers rather than uphold the principles of free competition and the protection of consumer rights.

Regulation was conceptually and normatively bolstered by claims that the industry was 'contestable', with absence of entry and exit barriers, potentially easy exits and switches on the part of customers among carriers, and lesser ability of incumbents to quickly react to other incumbents' and new entrants' moves.[7] It was not actual competition per se but rather the potential threat of such competition that was feared, not the least by existing operators. Therefore, in the 1960s, when state-owned national carriers controlled the industry, among the justifications for retaining the inherited regulatory regime was the risk of destructive competition. Additional concerns were gradually added to the list of objections to deregulation, including the alleged inability of existing businesses to adapt at short notice to rapid changes in demand, in the presence of high fixed costs. Thus, regulation was seen as the only viable solution to potential market failures[8] – a key argument also found in strands of game theory which had adopted the so-called 'core theory'. According to proponents of this thesis, liberalisation and the strong competition generated by it within the air transport industry would be incapable of guaranteeing a stable long-term equilibrium. In the case of 'empty core' – an oligopolistic market with no price equilibrium – the quantity supplied surpasses demand, forcing some operators to exit the market, reducing supply and increasing the market price. Such claims may be problematic, since it is only through price wars that individual market shares can be maintained, potentially destroying the industry or reducing product or service quality. The only solution to an 'empty core' situation seems to be for businesses to strike agreements in order to fix prices or the quantities supplied.

In spite of theoretical and normative arguments favouring this status quo and the political support for it, the cumbersome and overly bureaucratic system of approvals, subsidies, controls and delays was already under pressure in the 1970s, and arguments were mounting against its inefficiencies and escalating costs. In October 1978, one of the first steps towards liberalising and freeing up this industry was taken, by signing the Airline Deregulation Act in the USA. Although some residual control over the industry was to be maintained, through the operation of the US FAA, government supervision and surveillance were relaxed or removed in a number of key areas such as routes, fares and entry into the industry. Not long after the Act was passed, conflicts with labour union escalated, as did the number of bankruptcies and liquidations. However, heightened competition also accelerated the growth of the hub-and-spoke model of air travel, the arrival of new competitors, and the dramatic fall of fares, and encouraged higher capacity utilisation as well as greater responsiveness to the specific needs of individual markets, including convenience for airline customers. These early deregulation and liberalisation steps in the US heralded similar, though slightly later, changes in Europe, Asia and Latin America.

The effect of deregulation was rather different in Europe, prior to the arrival of customer compliance businesses. Although prices generally declined even before 1997 (during the first phase of European deregulation which was initiated in December 1992), fares on European destinations were still higher than those on comparable routes and distances in the US in the late 1990s, and many carriers had remained state-owned. In fact, throughout the 1990s, and in spite of the initial steps taken to relax industry controls, barriers of a strategic nature were erected by a number of European incumbents, in an attempt to maintain existing market positions and shares.[9] Such developments suggest that the contestable market theory may not be entirely applicable, at least not in its pure theoretical form, to the air transport industry. As far as post-1997 liberalisation of the European airline industry is concerned, it created new dynamics in this competitive field. Unlike the outcomes of pre-1997 deregulation, developments in the 2000s which were spurred by the opening up of national markets did not lead to the entry of competitors similar to those that had already populated the market.[10] Instead, many new arrivals actively sought novel solutions – different from the business models developed over past decades by national airlines. New entrants looked elsewhere for strategy and marketing inspiration, being eager to learn from the experience of Southwest Airlines in the USA and thus paving the way for the growth of what become to be known as the European low-cost airlines – some of the premier examples of customer compliance businesses, as will be explained in later sections.

In banking and financial service provision, governmental oversight was similarly, and gradually, relaxed during the period studied here. As in the case of the airline industry, liberalisation did not denote the complete and wholesale withdrawal of controls and supervision, but aimed at reducing the number and complexity of governmental mandates, with a view to increasing competition, growing the industry and therefore the economy, and benefiting customers. The origins of industry regulations are found in 1930s legislative measures. The Glass-Steagall Act of 1933, also known as the Banking Act of 1933, had been passed in order to – among other considerations – control speculation. The Act, along with additional prohibitions, was to ensure that distinct bank types were to be kept separate, that conflicts of interest were to be controlled, and that bank deposits were going to be insured through the Federal Deposit Insurance Corporation. Pressures on the Act mounted in the late 1970s and continued throughout the 1980s. The US banking industry actively lobbied for relaxation of controls, seeking to repeal this piece of 1933 legislation. This was finally achieved in 1999 with the passing of the Gramm-Leach-Bliley Act which liberalised the market by opening it to a number of distinct financial service entities, by relaxing existing controls over consolidation, and by repealing the above mentioned prohibitions over conflicts of interest in the industry. In the past decade, financial providers have taken advantage of these relaxations, with investment banks, traditional banks and insurance companies entering each other's market and offering a host of new banking products – a development which is incidentally credited by some for the recent financial meltdown and the current recession.

Elsewhere, deregulation in the electricity sector created a new breed of generators, and relaxed the rules of competition, freeing up space for the birth of new 'populations' of competitors – thus providing empirical support for Robinson's[11] incorporation of 'dramatic changes in market structures' and 'organizational forms' among the major effects of deregulation and the liberalisation of markets. Similar outcomes have been reported in other sectors where customer compliance businesses have become prominent more recently. Communications and telecommunications, for instance, have long been marked by regulatory relaxation, partly driven by rapid technological changes which regulatory regimes have struggled to handle and contain. Developments in communications and computer technology have rapidly and exponentially augmented the number and variety of communications offers, services and solutions, both to businesses and end consumers. Following the Telecommunications Act of 1996 in the US, which repealed or amended parts of the 1934 Communications Act, companies which had previously operated in separate segments of the market could compete directly. Service offerings were deregulated, and price controls were relaxed. Largely as a reactive response to technological innovations, this new laissez-faire and pro-business approach allowed, for instance, landline operators to offer wireless products, and media cross-ownership was legalised.

---

**Section summary for managers:**

o *Privatisation and deregulation have transformed the landscape of many sectors in recent years, including transport, banking and financial services, education, health services, utilities and many services previously provided by the public and third sectors.*

o *Such changes provide opportunities to innovate, compete differently, and be rid of past monopolistic practices.*

o *New entrepreneurial businesses have taken advantage of such regulatory changes, implementing innovative business models which underpin competitive success. Often, such competitiveness is achieved through some form of making customers and business partners compliant.*

---

## 2.2   Technological drivers of customer compliance

Although economic and regulatory changes of the type described above can be credited for the arrival of customer compliance businesses in recent years, it is technological innovations that have enabled these businesses to a greater extent, providing them with a distinct advantage over less entrepreneurial incumbents. Technology drivers of customer compliance have assumed different forms, each of them facilitating and accelerating differently the arrival and growth of customer compliance as a distinct way of rethinking one's relations with customers and other constituencies. Underlying such differences, though, is the general effect that new technological solutions have had on competition and novelty in marketing thinking. It suffices to remind ourselves that electronic commerce, for example, has accelerated existing commercial trends and has induced novel ways of conducting business, co-ordinating work and interacting in society.[12] These it has achieved by enabling new business models, re-shaping existing relations, nurturing new types of exchanges, and contributing to changes in market structure. As a result, the nature of competition and competitive advantage has been radically altered.

We open the discussion of technological changes and their impact on competition with recent developments in call-centre technologies, many of which are extensively used by customer compliance businesses in managing their relations with customers. Telephone interactions between customers and businesses have been standard practice ever since the telephone became a household item. However, grouping relatively minimally trained and low-cost call centre operatives into a single office, using PBX exchange systems to route calls, and relying heavily on pre-prepared scripts during interactions with customers, are relative new developments in business practice, having appeared only in the 1970s in the US and Europe. Companies also adopted the Interactive Voice Response, routing calls to specialist operatives – known as skills-based routing – and automatic distribution of calls to staff. Using such technology-driven systems of automation and centralising all types of telephone contact in one location were welcomed by managers, for technology solutions appeared to reduce costs, simplify customer interaction management and relieve technical staff of seemingly mundane duties when being interrupted by telephone calls and simple customer enquiries.

More recently, and once more driven by advances in telephony, computers and microchip-enabled call switching, call centre management has developed further. These days it is software driven and almost fully automated. Computers and automated call-management systems handle the initial interaction with customers, by verifying their identity not only for security reasons but also to provide information on pre-recorded messages and encourage callers to use other automated vehicles of customer communications and relationship management, such as the provider's website. Automation of both types is an increasingly important source of information for companies about customers and their behaviours. It also resolves queries effectively while also monitoring various aspects of calls much more efficiently than call-centre operatives and other human agents.

Automation of call-centre operations has been advanced by the arrival of sophisticated database management software and databases which are made up of data fields containing information on individual customers, records and lists.[13] Compiled and transmitted in a digitalised format, such lists are easily transferable and exchangeable, and are readily comparable and combinable with other lists for purposes of automated data analysis and automated customer relationship management. In terms of patterns of database use, companies are no longer satisfied with basic data entries about individual customers, including geo-demographic information or accounts of past interactions with customers. Rather, for purposes of successful data mining and effective customer management initiatives, the value of data are in the detail.[14] In the Internet age, databases contain not only customer contact details and past purchase information but elements of 'intensive customer intelligence' which contains historical records about buying and search habits, as well as real-time clickstream information allowing for interactive predictive modelling of customer preferences.[15] With ever more powerful computers and increasingly sophisticated software available to businesses, database-focused customer management has entered the 'high-dimensional formats' age,[16] where tens of thousands of data fields on individual customers can be easily produced, connected, communicated and used for purposes of channelling the behaviour of individuals at low cost and to the advantage of the service providers.

Searching for, combining and making sense of data and information owned by companies illustrate the value of new technologies to a variety of businesses these days. Companies such as Autonomy use ready systems or develop proprietary software to mine data fields, by accessing and assessing information held in different types of formats by businesses, including text documents, e-mails, voice messages as well as the data held in conventional databases. Autonomy – a company which was valued at GBP 7.2 bn (USD 11.7 bn) in August 2011 and which recently sold its proprietary software to

Hewlett Packard – describe what they do in terms of 'meaning based com-puting', 'meaning based governance' and 'meaning based marketing', the latter being of greatest interest to this book, as it describes the manner in which new technology is embraced by businesses in order to 'understand', automate and rationalise information sense-making, for purposes of more effective and efficient decision making. Successful companies like Autonomy provide the technology needed by customer compliance businesses, by addressing the latter's requirements for software which analyses automati-cally unstructured data held in different areas and functions of a business. Such software tends to revolutionise data mining and real-time analysis, and alters the nature not only of relations with customers but also of market and marketing research.

While call centre technologies, data management and data mining soft-ware have played a part in the growth of the emerging digital economy – also referred to as innovation, knowledge, new or e-economy – it is not so much the role of ICT sectors and their effect on providers such as the customer compliance businesses studied by us but the input of the Internet and the growth of Internet-based businesses, also known as e-commerce, that deserve one's attention. The birth of the Internet can be traced back to develop-ments in the USA in the 1950s and 1960s, including solutions in areas of point-to-point communications and packet switching. The description and assessment of disparate developments in protocols and networks between the 1960s and 1990s are beyond the scope of this book. However, regard-ing the commercial effect of the Internet more generally and its impact on the businesses titled here customer compliance, momentous proved to be the decommissioning of NSFNET in 1995. This marked the start of the commercialisation of the Internet – the point in time when restrictions on commercial traffic over the Internet were relaxed. Thus, although the com-mercial potential of this technology had already been realised by some in the 1990s,[17] with academics and practitioners foreseeing the fundamental transformations that information technologies could unleash in efficiency enhancement and market structure coordination,[18] it has been only in the last decade or so that e-commerce has grown.

E-commerce is thriving, driven by attempts to cut costs, enrich service offers, and reduce time. It is energised by new generations of powerful com-puter networks that enable distant exchanges between buyers and sellers and provide support during pre-purchase, purchase and post-purchase interactions alike. Single businesses as well as entire industries have grown, largely thanks to the migration of customers from face-to-face, to call centre, to Internet interactions, in their search for information, service delivery, support and solutions. Instructive is the case of the online auction industry which 'owes it' entirely to the Internet and e-commerce.[19] Exemplary is also the evolution of early customer compliance businesses in air transportation and financial service provision, from call centre-based companies to Internet-enabled pro-viders. Companies have embraced automated customer interactions whereby customers communicate with the company through its website. Those customers who face difficulties in using Internet-based communication channels tend to be viewed as economically costly and may even be discouraged by such providers.

---

**Section summary for managers:**

o *Electronic commerce has accelerated existing commercial trends and introduced novel ways of conducting business.*
o *Telephone and online interactions with customers are the norm in many sectors. Dedicated call centres use minimally trained and low-cost staff frequently operating in low-wage areas of the world.*
o *Call centres utilise automated back-office software, aimed at reducing the cost of service provision, partly by making customers compliant.*
o *Companies are constantly seeking lower-cost methods to provide customer service, web-based self-help systems being a prime example.*
o *Technology acts as a key driver of customer compliance whereby companies using new technology solutions have re-designed relationships with their customers.*

---

## 2.3  Examples of new businesses capitalising on regulatory, economic and technological changes

Although Robinson has identified one aspect of organisational change resulting from deregulation (the mergers and alliances that have followed liberalisation in the studied sectors), in this book, we describe a completely new organisational form. Commentators such as Dyck and Reinbergs (1998) who note the difficulties faced by established players in redefining themselves and in taking advantage of deregulation have thus failed to recognise the single most important effect of deregulation and technological developments in terms of changes in existing organisational populations and the birth of new populations. Having become firmly established in their respective markets, some customer compliance businesses have themselves accelerated more recently the further deregulation and liberalisation of markets.

A number of regulation-induced and technology-driven features of customer compliance businesses are readily identifiable. Businesses have profited extensively from deregulation. In fact, as noted above, their arrival is largely attributable to the opening up of sectoral environments. Among easyJet's innovative initiatives aimed at retaining low costs are tight control of selling, administrative and fixed costs, short turnaround times, operating a flat company structure with minimum permanent staff, and the use of less popular and smaller airports.[20] Of these, the last initiative marks a dramatic departure from the operations of pre-deregulation airlines, and would not have been possible before the late 1990s.

Market liberalisation and the relative ease of crossing national and market boundaries these days also account for the phenomenal success of yet another customer compliance business – IKEA. Many of IKEA's innovative practices in areas of retailing, sourcing and logistics would have had a lesser impact on retailing and the furniture market, or may not have been as successfully implemented, under pre-liberalisation conditions.

Sophisticated new technologies also fuel the competence with which customer compliance businesses such as eBay continuously introduce additional services to its customers, such as the 'buy-it-now', 'want-it-now', and 'best offer' features. In fact, eBay is known primarily for 'making headlines' not only for its market leadership or its innovative model as an online auction site and an electronic middleman but its technological and 'consequently' product ingenuity, including novel ways of communicating within and to the brand community, member feedback and search capabilities.

However, regarding technology-powered aspects of customer compliance operations, first and foremost is the heavy investment on the part of these businesses in databases. Irrespective of whether they are built internally or bought, databases form the backbone of the marketing efforts of customer compliance businesses and are among the premier explanatory factors of the growth of these companies. Amazon collects considerable information about its customers, which ends up in the company databases. Far from being used as 'narrow tools' for specialist direct marketing,[21] data and database management are key to managing customer relations not only because of their capacity to increase customer responsiveness and accountability as well as personalise such contacts,[22] but also due to their ability to help companies channel and control customer behaviour, as will be explained in our account of service provision innovations designed and implemented by customer compliance businesses. In light of such centrality of data, databases and database management to customer relationship management of customer compliance businesses, it is not surprising that data quality is a key issue and has attracted the attention of managers and external commentators of these companies. A holistic approach to data management tends to be adopted. Unlike many traditional businesses that struggle to effectively collect, update, absorb and utilise data,[23] customer compliance businesses appear to have fewer, if any, problems in terms of data quality management, data accuracy and accessibility, and its currency, as well as data quality measurement and improvement,

Server storage, Internet and telecommunication advances have dramatically reduced data storage, transmission, and application costs, and have thus encouraged database marketing and data management as part of ordering and fulfilment undertaken by customer compliance businesses. Such costs have fundamentally altered the nature of service provision and especially service recovery and complaint management practices of these companies. Call centre and online interfaces are presented typically as a series of forms or decision trees which feed into, while building upon, company databases. These forms and decision tress are completely or partially inflexible, from the point of view of customers, in that they require the completion of highly detailed instructions and the provision of specific information. During online interactions and, less so, call centre exchanges, customers are also expected to complete the required transactions, often on their own. The data are then processed by back-room computers utilising automated software systems or cloud servers physically located outside the business. Customer self-entry of data not only increases data accuracy and currency. The whole process is highly cost effective, but also producing a traceable order trail. Customers are basically compelled to carry out the work previously undertaken internally by clerical staff. With software becoming more sophisticated, such increased automation predicated on data collection and management is likely to increase, in spite of reservations in academic circles, for stored data can be easily and automatically analysed to profile individual customers, their tastes, needs and requirements.

In an increasingly competitive environment, many organisations see customer service as key to achieving and sustaining competitive advantage. Often this is part of a broader CRM approach that is concerned with developing synergistic relationships with customers. It seems that many customer compliance businesses have achieved this through their success in managing relations with customers by using latest technology. Service recovery too has been automated, with the resulting standardisation of service recovery processes, often devoid of human interaction. Automation not only reduces costs of addressing service failure in this manner but also seems to act as a sieving mechanism whereby unwanted customers are dissuaded from doing business with the company.

---

### Chapter summary for managers:

o *Privatisation, deregulation and technological advances are the main drivers of the birth and dramatic growth of customer compliance and customer-compliance-practising businesses.*

o *Innovative back-office software and new technology have replaced face-to-face service provision with technology-mediated interactions which are a key feature of customer compliance.*

o *Automated back-office software, for instance used to direct operatives in call centres, offers higher levels of customer satisfaction while also enforcing company rules and systems of interaction.*

o *The very nature of online and call-centre interactions has been altered, whereby customers have come to expect and accept standardised procedures and inflexible processes of interaction with companies which force customers to comply with company expectations and service-interaction demands.*

# 3   The Technology and its Applications

## 3.1   Data, data management and database marketing

---

**Key questions in this chapter:**

o *Are your company website, call centre and other customer interaction systems integrated in your overall strategy, or does your company treat them as peripheral, less important or add-ons?*

o *Does your business seek to reduce costs of interactions with customers, for instance by using new technology and making customers compliant while meeting their needs and wants?*

o *How much importance does your business place on data, databases, database marketing, call centre and Internet-based service solutions? How valuable are your databases?*

---

Only the more relevant technological innovations and key technological applications used by customer compliance businesses are reported and assessed here. Emphasis is placed on the nature and role of data, databases, database marketing, call-centre technologies and Internet-related technology solutions, more specifically the design and use of websites for customer relationship management driven by very innovative back-office software.

Academic literatures have long been intrigued by the importance of data, databases and database marketing to businesses which compete by applying modern communication systems and technology solutions. An up-to-date, accurate and complete database has become central to offering one-to-one marketing which would have been possible in the past only by personally knowing customers or by using laborious manual systems. Building databases, frequently of millions of customers by capturing and using hundreds of pieces of information on each individual customer, is a priority for most customer compliance businesses discussed here. Companies such as eBay, Amazon, Google and Ryanair have outcompeted their rivals and have become dominant operators in their sectors, greatly due to the extensiveness and quality of data as well as the effective harnessing of such data for decision-making purposes. For many such businesses, databases constitute much of the value of the company, with some such companies having little in the way of tangible assets apart from unique in-house software.

Spencer-Matthews and Lawley[1] are among many academic and business commentators who have noted the role of customer databases to modern organisations. They actually describe databases as a requirement for any successful organisation,[2] as part of a description of the growth of database marketing from a narrow tool, used for specialist direct mail and direct marketing campaigns, to a widely applied technology solution with company-wide implications for managing relations with customers. Database marketing provides much value to organisations, due to its unique capacity to personalise contacts, improve responsiveness, and increase accountability.[3]

As previously mentioned, businesses have maintained customer records long before the arrival of the technological solutions described in this chapter. Many companies across sectors have traditionally held datasets of customer accounts – among the first business areas to become computerised. Business proprietors and their staff knew their customers personally, including their preferences and dislikes. Such preferences were often memorised, noted and commented upon in written business records, allowing providers to match company offerings with specific customer needs. However, such data management attempts tended to be effective only with respect to a restricted number of customers, and they usually covered a limited geographical area only, where people knew one another personally.

More recently, data were at the heart of the operations of mail-order catalogue businesses. These came to dominate the supply of goods, especially those goods that were not readily available in a locality. Thomas Chippendale's 'The Gentleman and Cabinet-Maker's Director' in 1762 was essentially a mail-order catalogue of his furniture. At the time, 'The Director' would have been a very expensive book to print but was still economically viable for as a sales aid. In USA, Benjamin Franklin was among the pioneer cataloguers when he published a catalogue of scientific and academic books in 1744. However, it was not until Sears, Roebuck and Co. and Montgomery Ward that mail-order companies became firmly established. In the late 1870s, these businesses started offering goods at lower prices than those in local stores. It did not take long for what today we refer to as direct marketing to emerge. Due to their ability to sell directly to customers and because of their large buying power, mail-order companies sold at considerably lower prices than establishments with long supply chains. Sears, Roebuck and Co. website comments that 'Thanks to volume buying, to the railroads and post office, and later to rural free delivery and parcel post, they offered a happy alternative to the high-priced rural stores' – an argument that is applicable to modern online e-commerce sites as well. Early mail-order companies innovated also by maintaining databases of their customers, typically managed manually by armies of clerks. As sales volumes and businesses grew, though, some businesses introduced a certain level of automation to their data management activities. These companies were also among the first to profile their customers in a more professional manner and not too dissimilarly from what was to become the norm in marketing. They pioneered and applied solutions that were counterintuitive to marketing thinking at the time, not the least by offering catalogues with higher prices to their best customers while sending catalogues at lower prices to those who had not ordered.

In the early 1990s, at the outset of e-commerce, practitioners keenly interested in database management tended to equate it with direct mail and catalogue selling. Meanwhile, some researchers had already initiated the heated debates about data mining and database-driven customer profiling that were to mark the next decade or so of academic enquiry. More recently, and following advances in automation and computerisation of customer data management, database marketing has come to signify the building, organising, supplementing and mining of customer transaction databases, with the sole purpose of enhancing the accuracy of marketing thinking and fulfilment efforts.[4] Recent and current developments in database marketing have been paralleled, and much affected, by the growth of loyalty card schemes, some of the earliest of which were issued by retailers in an attempt to collect and assess information about purchasing habits and customer preferences. Retailers realised that good quality information and the automation of its collection, processing and use could enhance business effectiveness and competitive advantage. High-quality customer data thus became key to retail success.

Emphasis is increasingly being placed on data quality and data management concerns. Data quality, for instance, is an issue which has attracted much attention on the part of customer management practitioners and academics working in the area. There have been a number of high-profile failures of customer relationship management projects, and many of these have been blamed on poor data quality and management. With research on this issue growing both in academic outlets and in the business press, analysts have detected and commented upon the incomplete and inaccurate data retained by many major businesses in developed economies. Various aspects of data, datasets, databases and database management have proved to be of inadequate quality, including data appropriateness, inaccuracy, and inaccessibility. Problems have also been reported with much data being invalid, verified only superficially or not verified at all and not being updated regularly. Users have little confidence in certain categories of data collected by big organisations.

Sources of inadequate data have been identified by Cutter Consortium. These include poor data entry, missing data across database fields, overlapping databases, obsolete and poorly presented data in older systems and a lack of company-wide data management standards. Furthermore, few companies seem to take account of these problems when planning their CRM (Customer Relationship Management) projects, and data quality complications often do not become apparent until the project is underway.[5] Similarly, survey results reported by Spencer-Matthews and Lawley[6] further illustrate the extent of ineffective generation, sharing, management and use of data. Glitches seem to be much deeper and considerably more systemic in North America. For instance, a large majority of surveyed organisations admitted that company systems could not recognise and welcome customers. Only slightly more than half of the companies demonstrated 'good use of customer data' or had specialist resources in support of data management. Less than a third seemed to have customer information plans in place or had developed incentives for supporting data quality management. In conclusion, the authors of the report expressed their dissatisfaction with the findings, suggesting that such results were not impressive. This assessment was backed by discoveries of less than adequate customer databases even in client business-to-business organisations. Management often did not seem to treat data software issues as challenges facing their companies and requiring urgent attention.

In their critical assessment of data quality improvement activities, Henderson and Murray[7] have focused on the importance of data content and architecture as two sources of customer management excellence. They state that data content and its architecture affect data quality and the extent to which data are fully utilised as part of customer management. Techniques for assessing organisational capabilities in terms of data sourcing, management and use are presented, including what the authors term 'vicious' or 'virtuous' circles of customer data. Data usage can be ineffective or incomplete, for instance in cases of missing or low-quality data on corporate structures. Missing or 'sub-optimal' use of data limits, in turn, organisational ability to update records.

Certain companies have realised that data management problems such as those described above present distinct competitive opportunities, and that a holistic approach to data management is required alongside a strategic methodology of collecting personalised data founded upon cross-functional integration.[8] Academics have contributed much to such a realisation, having urged businesses to attend to data quality and data management challenges. Until relatively recently, academics have also been voicing their concern about the lack of research and understanding in this area. To academics like Jenkinson,[9] organisational success is driven by a shared understanding, among company employees and management, of the importance of data. Corporate data warehouses, it has been suggested, need to be integrated, and IT personnel should be closely involved in customer management decision making.

As a result of the above-mentioned problems and the realisation of the gravity of the challenges they posed to businesses, a new generation of companies has arisen which write or market software allowing data mining to be carried out across a whole range of formats, including differently formatted databases, texts such as e-mails and letters and even recorded voicemail held by companies. The growth in the number and variety of companies that offer solutions to data and database management problems has been considerable, and some are currently highly valuable enterprises. One such example is the sale in August 2011 of Autonomy.com to HP for a reported USD 11.7 bn – illustrating the value which many businesses now place on the importance of storing, cleaning, updating, analysing and using in-house data.[10] However, although data quality problems appear to have been alleviated, further improvements are required. As Spencer-Matthews and Lawley[11] note, the situation seems to have improved in the past decade or so. However, they also felt that it has taken businesses the best of 15 years to get where they currently are with respect to data management, database management and data quality management. Surveyed business could hardly be complacent, they conclude.

Many customer compliance businesses studied here appear to have appreciated the importance of high-quality data and database management. The crucial role that data integration plays in database management is also understood, with company-wide systems often managed by senior executives. Data management is approached as a strategic issue by such companies. No department seems to 'own' the data, and few, if any, examples of firewalling data and information from the organisation as a whole can be uncovered. Organisations recognise that data stored in their in-house databases is a valuable asset, and couple the building and extending of such databases with a comprehensive data management strategy, put in place in order to implement successful customer relationship management initiatives. Any problems with data storage, database management and database marketing are typically addressed within enterprise-wide initiatives, backed by enterprise-wide solutions which also help resolve problems related to ownership of integrated customer databases.

Traditional businesses against which customer compliance businesses compete have developed their datasets and databases over many years. They may be burdened by various, often conflicting, vested interests. In some cases, the redesign of fragmented and disputed data management systems is costly or impossible, often requiring the implementation of completely new strategic plans. Such change initiatives tend to be difficult, costly and time-consuming endeavours which are also typically challenging to implement. Additional challenges stem from the propensity of a few traditional businesses to adopt a micro perspective on data and data management issues, with insights at the tactical level of decision making being much more prevalent – fuelling comments such as Cooper's[12] that many companies tend not to make the most of the data collected and available in their databases. Descriptions such as Cooper's are easily contrasted with the more holistic and strategic approach to automation more generally, and to data management in particular, among the companies referred to as customer compliance businesses which not only tend to build powerful internal databases but also integrate more effectively multiple sources of information as a source of their accurate understanding of their customer base.

The distinction among data, information and knowledge – or data, knowledge and insights – is instructive of different methods and outcomes of decision making between traditional and customer compliance businesses. Whereas the focus of many academics, business analysts and companies had tended to be on data (that is, the raw material that awaits processing), customer compliance businesses have emphasised the derivation of regularities from such raw material possessed by companies. Therefore, emphasis is placed on information and, even more so, knowledge, or the expectations that customer compliance businesses come to accumulate about their customers, based on the information contained in internally held, integrated datasets. The cost of obtaining raw data on which marketing activities rely has been reduced, with customer compliance businesses expecting and often even forcing their customers (making them 'compliant') to supply the data during purchasing, ordering, returns, and when lodging complaints. With automation applied to all of the above-mentioned activities but also with respect to analysis and utilisation of such data – for instance, through data mining – the time and cost to capture data, turn it into information and analyse such information are dramatically reduced. In fact, with new software and even more powerful computers available to businesses these days, this can be done in real-time and almost instantly.

Success in data management is predicated on customer compliance businesses treating data as a distinct and separate asset, and not a resource in the possession of their IT departments. Data on customers, transactions, products, outlets, interactions, fulfilment and service recovery tends to be centrally held and centrally managed. Ownership and management of data are treated as the responsibility of senior management. Business functions and decision making seem to be computerised in a piecemeal fashion, and data storage is not seen as a mainly technological matter of tactical importance. Nor are data held across incompatible databases and organisational divisions which typically operate as separate company silos which rarely engage in synergistic decision making.

This highly structured approach to collecting, accessing, assessing, integrating and using data starts at the very point of entry of new pieces of data. Customer compliance businesses use a number of strategies to make customers conform to data entry expectations, by compelling them to 'work with' company systems. This largely ensures that the data entered by customers are accurate and current – offering in turn distinct advantages to the customer compliance business model, to be discussed in later chapters of the book. Carefully designed website forms, used extensively by these companies, ensure that data are corrected at the point of entry, even preventing customers from gaining access to the company's products and services unless complete and correct data are entered by customers, with little to no input from the company. Similar in nature are the call centre and face-to-face interactions with company personnel, whereby compliance procedures are applied, not least to coerce callers to supply as much valuable information as possible, at little marginal cost to the company. Thus, compliance techniques are used when communicating with customers but also with staff and business partners to supply data freely, according to data capture and data entry standards preset by the customer compliance business. It is not uncommon for automated back-office software to prevent customers from proceeding with their queries, purchases or browsing activities unless data are entered in the exact format required by the business. Data entry standards and requirements are extensive and carefully prescribed. Deviations are typically not tolerated in such automated interactions, ensuring data quality and accuracy. Perhaps even more important, from the point of view of effective and efficient data management, is the effect that such procedures have on data standardisation; for non-deviation on the part of customers also ensures that the collected data will be supplied to the customer compliance business in the expected, standardised format.

A relatively simple example is the manner in which customers visiting the website of a customer compliance business are expected to enter their postcode, or zip code. Usually, the company website clearly specifies the format in which the address and the postcode need to be presented. In order to further standardise this crucial piece of data and thus assist decision making, customers are often presented with a ready list of options. Such rigidity in data provision ensures that the correct address will be added to the company's database and that it will be entered in a format which minimises delivery and mistakes. Standardised, accurate, high-quality data which are held in one internal database or across databases which freely communicate with one another can be easily collected, combined, recombined and subjected to sophisticated analysis. Consequently, customer compliance businesses tend to profit from the cheap and quick detection of trends and the production of summative analyses on significant aspects of consumer behaviour. Such data can be analysed automatically, and the results are used to introduce changes such as altering the flow of traffic or modifying the pricing or other aspects of offers.

Unlike traditional offline systems of data collection and management, which require ongoing training and assistance of customer management staff, ensuring data quality is easier and cheaper when undertaken through automated systems. Automation is also exercised with respect to customer browsing patterns, orders placed, payment details, customer complaints and service recovery incidents. The most sophisticated software systems can access all data fields pertaining to an individual customer, and can compile and combine the data into instant reports. Software is also used to match data against standardised lists. Methods of automatically searching internal databases have improved, including in cases where information has been entered using different, even incompatible, formats. Databases can be cross-checked, and incompatible or outdated data pieces are easily and more cheaply eliminated. Importantly, customer compliance businesses often ask customers to carry out many of these data quality actions themselves.

The reported difficulties in compiling and effectively using data and databases that we briefly assessed at the start of this discussion on novel technology solutions may need to be linked to more general problems that many companies have in applying new technologies to the customer end of the supply chain[13] and to strategic decision making.[14] Customer compliance businesses appear to have reduced or, at times, resolved altogether such technology-application challenges. By achieving this, they demonstrate the benefits of using technology to its full potential. Such success is at least partly attributed to the fact that many such organisations are recent arrivals and have grown as new entrepreneurial companies which have not been inhibited by multiple and incompatible datasets and databases, inherited systems, staff unwilling to change, sclerotic cultures and organisational structures.

---

### Section summary for managers:

o *A lot has been written about the importance of data and the positive effect of databases and database management on company performance. Many companies seem not to treat data that they possess on their customers as a distinct, valuable asset.*

o *Some businesses cannot effectively update, integrate and use data, information and knowledge held in departmental databases in a strategic fashion for purposes of planning, logistics, stock control, sales and marketing, as well as managing customer service.*

o *Customer compliance businesses appear to have resolved problems of maintaining and managing databases by forcing customers to enter data correctly check and update such data. Much of the data on sales and service contacts are recorded automatically and some are available for the customer to view and update.*

---

## 3.2   Call-centre technology and its use by customer compliance businesses

Call centre technology appears to play an important role in customer management strategies of the customer compliance businesses. This may be due to the fascination of these businesses with the application of standard operating procedures during exchanges with customers. Call centre technology and call centres applying such technology solutions are thus preferred control tools whereby observation of customers and influencing them based on such observation and the knowledge accumulated through observation are built into service encounters where the behaviours of both customers and customer compliance business employees are constrained by 'external forces', including novel technology solutions.[15] Such practices demonstrate the need, on the part of analysts, to recognise the extent to which management and the market attempt to impose new 'interaction orders' and redraw the boundaries around customer service. Human interactions are automated. They are being increasingly replaced with a system of exchanges which academics describe as 'machine-like'.

Automation of customer interactions has been assisted by technical advances in telephony during the past 30 years, including the advent and application of computerised systems handling, storing, recording and switching landline telephone calls. Coupled with the earlier discussed deregulation, privatisation, the opening up of national markets and the resulting increase in competition among telecommunication operators, such technological advances have dramatically reduced the cost of phone calls. The traditional monopolies which used to control voice and data traffic have been broken up. This has further decreased costs, with the cost of phone calls halved almost every five years. Furthermore, new entrants have flooded the market. They have made substantial investments in new computerised technology services and infrastructure. Such developments have created opportunities for cost-effective ways to contact customers directly by telephone, and call centres using mainframe, microcomputers, LANs and integrated technology known as computer telephony integration (CTI) have grown in number and their sophistication in order to meet such new customer management demands.

Call centre contacts with the customers of customer compliance businesses may be executed through telephone calls, emails, online chat, websites and even instant messaging. The data collected through these methods of communication are both easily and cheaply tracked, and are recorded in databases as part of the company's customer relationship management. Customer compliance businesses have been among the first to apply some of the latest technologies in use for purposes of handling customer calls, including telephone keypad options, speech recognition software, text evaluation and natural language processing. Agent training appears to be paramount for automatic customer call handling. This includes the analysis of best practices from past interactions, in order to provide a better and more cost-effective service and also to ensure that complete, accurate and up-to-date data are collected on individual customers, as explained earlier. Operatives' performance is closely monitored, and crude measures such as number of calls handled per day have been abandoned in favour of more sophisticated metrics, including 'cost of incident successfully dealt with'. Adaptive systems based on clever software assisting call centre operatives are being gradually implemented, facilitating the swift and effective resolution of customer queries and problems. Such increasingly complex and innovative technologies and methods of interaction are often trialled and pioneered by customer compliance businesses.

While early call centres utilised private branch exchange (PBX) systems operated by companies, customer compliance businesses have been increasingly subcontracting these customer management services to large specialist providers. Large low-cost providers have grown in South Asia and South America, and they have built up considerable expertise in operating successful call centres, turning into leaders in the development, trialling and application of new technologies. Telephone systems of subcontracted organisations integrate with the systems of the client customer compliance businesses through public switched telephone network (PSTN) telephone lines or Voice over I P, by using the Internet. Data are recorded on automated systems and can be instantaneously used for research, marketing and CRM activities.

Call centres and the underlying technologies have attracted much criticism. They have been characterised as the modern equivalent of the industrial revolution satanic mills. Restrictive working practices, low pay, de-skilling, unsocial working hours, repetitiveness, high level of scripting of interactions and work-related stress induced by daily interactions with abusive customers have been widely documented in extant research. However, of greater interest to this discussion is the applicability of such criticisms to an understanding of compliance through call centre technology and interaction practices. Some compliance practices may have been 'accidental' in nature, especially in the early days of call-centre interactions, with the inadvertent exacting of obedience on the part of calling customers, for instance, due to mistakes in data handling and management on the part of the company. However, currently used systems have been perfected – they are deliberately designed to make calling customers comply with company expectations and procedures.

Control through technology solutions appears to affect customers and employees alike. For instance, the presentation of emotions on the part of call centre operatives tends to be pre-specified by the organisation and is embodied in rules of employment.[16] Employees are forced to follow narrowly scripted instructions.[17] Although variations have been observed in the nature and character of call centres, their principal objective is maximising customer throughput and minimising service delivery costs.[18] Performance monitoring of operatives is pervasive, and sophisticated computerised information systems are applied to capture data on number of calls answered, quality of interaction with customers, product knowledge of service providers and time spent away from the telephone in down time. With technology control being so pervasive and so extensively used, operatives are unable even to pace their own work.

However, as documented by Collin-Jacques[19] and Russell[20] in analyses of the design, adoption and utilisation of software programmes, call centre technologies and technology-enabled control are not immutable, as far as employees may be concerned. Flexibility with respect to specific decisions is often part of the technology platforms, whereby management may opt for increased employee input into the design features and deployment of the technologies in question. Therefore, in spite of widely reported pervasive technological and bureaucratic control,[21] total and totalising systems of observation and control[22] of operatives are often not entirely achievable. Because of the level of involvement of staff reported in some studies of call centres, it may be difficult to describe control as unavoidably total and totalising.

Customers seem to have adapted relatively quickly to using call centres, largely due to accessibility advantages. With increased consumer sophistication and growing time poverty, and in spite of perceptions of customer control during call centre interactions, contacting providers through their call centres is viewed as advantageous to the customers of customer compliance businesses. Technology mediated and extensively automated and controlled interactions through call centres greatly reduce the need for customers to travel, meet face to face company representatives, or fill in forms and wait in line. However, the underlying technologies also craft customers in new and unexpected ways. They structure and limit the choices and services available to customers, and extensively guide and channel customers' behavioural options and actual behaviours. Therefore, while it might be argued that customers have benefited from the accessibility of the call centre model, call centre technology also facilitates the successful application of customer compliance techniques. Within what could be best described as a machine model of customer service, service provision is rigidly controlled, with the aim of maximising efficiency and turning the allegedly sovereign consumer into an observed and controlled subject.

---

### Section summary for managers:

o *Call centre operatives working for customer compliance businesses are forced to follow prescribed procedures and company-sanctioned systems of interaction by following scripts appearing on computer screens.*

o *Multi-channel access to call-centres is common these days, using telephone keypads and voice recognition software which automates all but the most complex interactions.*

o *Call centre service provision is controlled by mid-level management in order to maximise efficiency and ensure the use of strict customer compliance systems and procedures of interaction with callers.*

---

## 3.3 Internet technological solutions and customer compliance

Internet-based service solutions have had a profound effect on competitors across sectors as well as the sectors themselves. Technological innovativeness has assumed different formats such as the provision of information to customers, communicating with and persuading customers, development of new distribution channels and disintermediation, and redistributing added value (see Figure 3.1), among others. Although the disintermediation effect noted in the figure was realised only in the early 2000s, it had been predicted by some visionaries such as Malone, Yates and Benjamin as far back as 1987 and other academics who foresaw the displacement of traditional intermediaries across value chains. To Porter, new technologies had the potential to transform the way in which business was conducted at the time. Electronic markets as those invented, trialled and currently utilised by many of the companies classified as customer compliance businesses have profoundly redefined the meaning of brokerage, by connecting sellers and buyers directly. Costs of attracting new e-customers have been dramatically reduced. Processes of attracting, communicating with and serving these e-customers have been 'liberated' from the complications and complexity associated with traditional face-to-face interaction processes. New progressive business models have been generated, altering the structure and very nature of entire business sectors.[23] Technology has turned into a powerful enabler of novel competitive marketing strategies.[24]

E-marketing or online marketing is actually among the newest developments in marketing theory and practice, following the development of the Internet less than two decades ago. Although its objectives are similar to those of earlier forms of marketing – that is, the identification and satisfaction of customer needs – this is achieved through electronic communication technologies. Thanks to e-marketing and e-commerce, most marketing activities can be planned and executed using online technology, accounting for the dramatic effect of the Internet on all aspects of marketing practice.[25] Some such examples include relationship marketing, marketing research, data mining, promotions and integrated marketing communications, supply chain management, sales and purchasing and after-sales support[26] as well as stock control and reordering. Much of the communication is automated, modified by complex algorithms built into the software systems and taking over functions previously undertaken by marketers. Thanks to such new technology applications, marketing has evolved from using one-way communication platforms to the application of interactive approaches, and customer relationship management systems have been redesigned through software packages which aid interactions between customers and providers, also enabling companies to deliver unified messages.

Many of the above-mentioned e-commerce principles, as those illustrated in Figure 3.1, were pioneered in the airline industry,[27] with the low-cost airlines incorporated in our list of customer compliance businesses pioneering many such innovations.[28] In order to cut down costs, customer compliance businesses have started offering electronic services and their promotional strategy and tactics emphasise online and website-based activities. Through the Internet, their customers can access information, browse service offers and promotions, register their preferences, make purchases, lodge complaints and provide other forms of feedback. More than 95 per cent of Ryanair tickets, for example, are booked online.[29]

Although much has been written about e-marketing and e-commerce, and in spite of accumulated knowledge about customer satisfaction in offline environments and traditional contexts of service provision,[30] the nature and role of customer satisfaction in online environments and during e-interactions have not been adequately studied. Furthermore, research on e-satisfaction tends to privilege the understanding of pre-purchase customer behaviour and

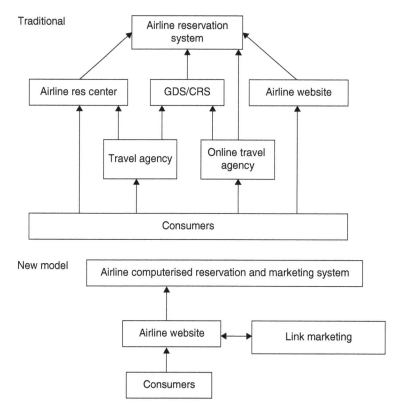

**Figure 3.1    Traditional and new distribution channels in air transportation**
Adapted from: Belobaba et al. (2009)

purchase-related decisions and interactions, at the expense of post-purchase experiences. Therefore, there is little in the way of knowledge about post-purchase e-satisfaction with service provision, and even less is known about how this relates to online complaint management, service recovery and the use of technology to control all or some groups of customers. Much of the e-commerce literature is devoted to the analysis of technological solutions available to practitioners, or business-model related aspects of competitiveness in this new environment. For instance, e-commerce business models have been identified and extensively discussed. Studies have also noted the role of new technology and technological applications to enhance customer service in electronic contexts.[31] Less research has been devoted, though, to uncovering and assessing after-sales service and interactions with customers, and especially e-service recovery and e-complaint management. In order to address these issues, the book will cover Internet-based technology solutions as well as the presence or absence of technology-mediated control, and the reactions of customers to such provider practices.

Of interest is the manner in which customer compliance businesses have utilised e-commerce to communicate with their customers and offer them

novel solutions, but also control them by making them compliant. In order
to investigate these matters, we offer an overview of some technological solutions which enable the marketing strategy behind customer compliance.

Website design has two components – technological design, and artistic
(graphic) and marketing design. Marketers use hypertext and hypermedia to con-
vert static web pages into dynamic, interactive platforms that present information
required by browsing viewers. Webpages are powered by various markup lan-
guages such as HTML and DHTML, along with ASP (Active Server Pages)
and JSP (JavaServer Pages). Increasingly important to website design is CMS
(content management systems) often using PHP scripts – a general-purpose
server-side scripting language originally designed for web development, to produce dynamic webpages. Software systems designed in the mid-1990s have
changed little; they are still the key ingredients of menu-driven, highly interactive websites. Much has been written on website layout – websites need to be
carefully planned, have clear objectives, and use simple layouts and technology
in order to achieve certain objectives. Graphic design elements should match the
functional objectives of a site, irrespective of the nature of the website as a 'bro-
chure website' or an 'e-commerce website'. Academics have designed long lists
of features and requirements for website design, and they have provided numerous examples of design failure. For instance, an e-commerce website for buying
and selling products, services and software should be simple, clear and easy to
use and navigate. However, e-commerce websites are generally more than retail
exchanges; they assist, and may even be central to, marketing, selling, product
delivery, customer care and market research.

Compliance through e-commerce solutions assumes various formats. By
the very nature of the Internet and Internet-enabled communication and
interaction processes designed by customer compliance businesses, interfaces
with customers tend to be very strictly prescribed, for example by using
online forms and tick boxes. Customers can rarely deviate from the sequence
of data input and data provision pre-designed by the provider, and cannot
enter information which does not fit pre-formatted boxes and fields. In some
cases, the pieces of data provided by customers are checked automatically
and almost instantaneously against information contained in the in-house
databases of the provider or merchant partners. A typical example is the
automatic checking of addresses against the Royal Mail PAF databases in
the UK. If the data provided by customers are incorrect or incomplete, or
are not supplied in the format required by the provider, the website software
forces customers to resubmit the data and thus comply with company rules
and expectations about data provision and data entry. Websites also incorporate pre-designed fields and tick boxes which are frequently activated following certain customers' actions. Populating fields and checking boxes also
typically precede certain customer actions. In order to proceed to checkout,
for instance, customers need to agree to the terms and conditions of the provider. All alterations to the procedures of the provider are executed through
the company software systems, and updated information is automatically
conveyed to employees and customers.

Recent developments in back-office software have further powered cus-tomer compliance, allowing such businesses to implement ever more stan-dardised and therefore effective and efficient systems of service provision through compliance, across all types of customer interfaces. The websites which have been discussed at such length by academics and business com-mentators are nothing more than customer interfaces, with back-office soft-ware actually being the 'brain' behind such compliance exchanges. It is the software that orchestrates interactions, for instance through the use of inter-active voice recognition applications (IVR) frequently used in the banking industry and customer compliance businesses elsewhere, automated helplines using IVR (Interactive Voice Response) technology and FAQ (Frequently Asked Questions) systems as a particularly prominent example of automated, control-laden type of customer support. While such examples of automation have been studied from an operational point of view, and the impact of auto-mation on the company's bottom line, this book examines the effect that they have had on customer-provider interfaces and their role in compliance practices.

Smart phones, PDAs (Personal Digital or Data Assistant), iPads and other devices need to be mentioned here as they seem to be growing in impor-tance to those customer compliance businesses working with the younger generation. Such technology solutions function by accessing the Internet in the same way as computers, using 3G mobile telephone technology. Mobile phones are used to contact call centres and may also become the preferred way to access the Internet in order to book travel and entertainment tick-ets, or access information and communicate with customer compliance businesses.

---

## Chapter summary for managers:

o *New technologies have transformed business models and strategies, in the process of doing so also highlighting the importance of data to modern businesses.*

o *Such technologies have dramatically reduced the costs of attracting custom-ers and communicating with them.*

o *Collecting, updating, transforming and harnessing data are central activities to customer compliance businesses, ensuring that accurate and up-to-date data and knowledge on customers are used to implement one-to-one auto-mated marketing.*

o *Market research, one-to-one marketing, service provision, service recovery, complaint management and pricing, among others, have been increasingly automated whereby individual needs are analysed and matched automati-cally, in many cases enabled through compliance systems of interaction.*

o *Call-centres and websites are two technology mechanisms where back-office software is designed to impose customer compliance procedures and thus reduce costs of service provision.*

# 4 New Forms of Service Provision

**Key questions in this chapter:**

o *Do you benchmark your marketing activities against latest innovations in managing relationships with customers?*
o *Are the interactions with your customers marked by customer centricity or do you use customer compliance strategies?*
o *For instance, how does your company handle service failure?*

## 4.1 What marketers do (and should be doing) according to marketing theory

Although contested by some marketing academics and practitioners, the majority of theorists in the discipline adhere to the view that marketing has passed through certain stages of development. According to this chronology, marketing and marketing management thinking and practice have progressed through stages of production and selling orientations before WWII, only to be replaced by two other concepts that have dominated thinking in marketing in the past few decades: the marketing concept and the relationship marketing concept. Most marketing academics accept that it is these two concepts that reflect most accurately current marketing practice and should also guide marketing managers.

There are competing interpretations of the origins and growth to dominance of the marketing concept. Nonetheless, we can accept that it can be traced to 1950s' normative claims that companies should place emphasis on the needs and wants of their customers.[1] Slightly earlier, Drucker[2] noted that marketing was not about selling only – a statement reaffirmed by Felton[3] and, later, by McNamara,[4] that the marketing concept denoted a state of mind or a philosophy founded on customer orientation, profit orientation and company-wide communication. A long line of studies since the 1950s has reaffirmed the centrality of this concept to marketing thinking, by refining and redefining it. Well known is the work of Kohli and Jaworski[5] where they list the contents of the concept, including customer orientation, coordinated marketing and profitability.

An aspect of the marketing concept beloved by theorists and espoused by many practitioners is customer orientation.[6] In keeping with the emphasis placed, as part of the marketing concept, on customers as the key stakeholder group to any business, customer orientation further deepens the marketers' belief in the central role that customers and their needs play, while noting, at least in theory, the importance to profitability of other stakeholders. In these times of increased competition, fast-paced change and growing complexity and unpredictability, with opening up of ever more sectors through liberalisation and privatisation, we are reminded that there are ongoing pressures to theorise about and practise customer centricity. Consequently, and not surprisingly, the growing literature on market orientation – commonly defined as the implementation of customer orientation[7] – has become yet another reincarnation of the marketing concept.

The strength and vitality of such thinking has been bolstered by the arrival some thirty years ago of yet another concept – relationship marketing.[8] Whereas marketing textbooks prefer to portray the marketing concept as a reaction to the hard sale tactics employed by businesses subscribing to the selling concept originating in the Great Depression, relationship marketing is commonly described as an extension, or an improvement, of the marketing concept. Its origins in the thinking of the Nordic school of services, the Swedish school of industrial marketing,[9] in theories of business-to-business (B2B) and channel management[10] and early studies of the industrial marketing and purchasing (IMP) group[11] help explain why so much emphasis is placed by proponents of relationship marketing on developing not only economic transactions but also social ties, on maintenance of relationships which are rewarding both to customers and providers[12] and on nurturing exchanges that remind readers of intimate, interpersonal links founded on trust, mutual understanding, communications and involvement. Supporters of relationship marketing seek to emphasise relations with all parties and not only with customers; however, in the process of creating 'relationship portfolios', which benefits all parties involved,[13] customer orientation and pleasing customers still dominate marketing thought.

Such thinking influences current texts on service provision, as part of service marketing – human productive activity which has been prominent across societies and in all phases of human history, yet one which has become particularly significant to developed economies, even if some thinkers have questioned its dominant role in modern society. Vargo and Lusch,[14] in their much acclaimed book on the service dominant logic, go further by arguing that service provision is integral to all sales propositions and that marketing all products is linked with, and defined by, service offers. Due to this importance of service provision to our economies and to the line of argument in this book, it is imperative to draw a link between service provision and relationship marketing thinking.

One should remember that relationship marketing originated, among others, in service marketing texts, and it was in this area that some of the earliest conceptual and empirical studies on building relationships with customers and business partners are found. For instance, one of the favourite topics in the service marketing literature is service quality, analysed in terms of technical and functional quality, or alternatively seen as the customers' overall assessment of their service experience.[15] Equally prominent are Parasuraman, Zeithaml and Berry's[16] dimensions of service encounters: tangibles, reliability, responsiveness, competence, courtesy, credibility, security, access, communication and understanding. Although they were subsequently reduced to the five dimensions of tangibles, reliability, responsiveness, assurance and empathy,[17] the thinking underlying the model has not changed. In fact, the 1988 modification has accentuated the assumptions of the marketing and relationship marketing concepts – the customer is the focus of both frameworks, and marketers' main task is to provide service as promised, accurately and dependably. Marketing practitioners are expected to develop and maintain a caring, individualised approach, being responsive to customer needs and demands, and treating customers with courtesy, in order to generate trust and win their confidence.

Assumptions and arguments of the 'early' services marketing literatures, as described above, still dominate marketing thinking and, allegedly, marketing practice. Throughout the 1990s and 2000s, marketers have studied and argued about service provision and especially service quality. They have compared customers' expectations with their actual experiences, and have invented and tested various strategies and tactics to increase customer satisfaction through service provision.[18] These days, practitioners are reminded that service is of 'strategic importance'[19] and that, consequently, it necessitates 'continual' 'enhancement' of the 'customer experience' and securing customers' 'satisfaction'.[20] Writings in academic and practitioner journals are equally emphatic when calling for and demanding satisfying customers and empowering them, for instance by involving them as 'co-producers' and by customising offerings that meet individual, unique needs.[21]

A sub-discipline in service marketing where these calls have been particularly vocal is service failure where academics have sought to gain an understanding of why and how service problems and mistakes occur.[22] Once service provision fails, service providers are expected to respond effectively by providing redress for the failure – referred to in marketing as service recovery.[23] To analysts, service recovery is a major opportunity for businesses to turn dissatisfied customers into satisfied ones and, as a result of their allegedly increased satisfaction, retain them as loyal business clients,[24] who are likely to spread positive feedback by word of mouth. Redress assumes various forms – businesses can provide monetary or non-monetary reimbursement such as an apology, or they may assist and even partially or completely compensate the customer for his or her inconvenience.[25] The literature expects, and advises practitioners, that the response of the lapsed provider should be quick, in order to encourage a positive customer's evaluation. Similarly, courteous and polite treatment of the customer during service recovery is assumed to be the norm.

The process and outcome of service recovery are strongly affected by the confirmation or disconfirmation of customers' expectations about the actions that the provider would take in order to rectify the mistake. Customers compare their expectations about service recovery with actual providers' responses to a failure, in order to form their post-recovery satisfaction or dissatisfaction. When and if the recovery exceeds the customer's expectations, one can talk about 'positive disconfirmation', while the reverse – 'negative disconfirmation' – may produce lasting dissatisfaction with a service provider.[26] Post-recovery evaluations on the part of the customer are also allegedly affected by the customer's perceptions of equity, by weighing the inputs (including the time and financial resources that the customer has spent resolving the failure, for instance by complaining) and outputs of transactions with that failed provider. Alternatively, post-recovery customers' evaluations have been shown to be associated with customers' perceptions of distributive, procedural and interactional fairness.[27] Distributive fairness concerns outcomes of service recovery and complaint management. We are told that if marketers offer their customers compensation, customers are likely to judge the recovery effort more favourably. However, if the compensation offered by the marketer is perceived as inadequate or if the customer's evaluation of procedural (referring to the policies, processes and rules of recovery efforts set by the provider) and interactional (describing interactions between customers and the service personnel in charge of managing complaints) fairness are low, post-recovery satisfaction is likely to suffer, consequently negatively affecting post-failure and post-recovery trust in the provider and the customer's commitment to his or her relationship with the provider.[28]

---

### Section summary for managers:

o *Marketing has passed through a number of stages in its development, and the evolution has accelerated since the advent of the Internet and other modern technologies.*

o *The marketing and relationship marketing concepts have been favoured by marketing theorists and practitioners during much of the twentieth century.*

o *We offer an analysis of latest trends in management practice, especially in relation to service recovery and complaint management, which question the universal applicability of marketing and relationship marketing concepts.*

---

## 4.2    What innovative marketers do … in practice

The brief review of current views in marketing about businesses' relationships with their customers demonstrates the strength of academics' convictions. Customers are almost invariably described as the single most important stakeholder group for any organisation. Without listening to them and pandering to their demands, it is suggested that businesses would not survive in today's climate of hyper competition. However, the businesses which we introduced in the opening of this book have questioned received wisdom in marketing thinking. Next we identify, conceptualise and empirically discuss a number of areas of marketing practice and service provision where these companies have invalidated much of what one reads in marketing texts. While it is in these areas that one finds key path-breaking practices, they do not exhaustively describe the innovative potential of these companies – it is a topic which we continue to discuss in the following chapters that address market and marketing research as well as strategic innovations of these businesses.

All aspects of innovative marketing practice and service provision of customer-compliance businesses rest on a highly distinct and possibly controversial view of customers, on the part of these companies, as well as on redefined relationships with customers. Although customers are still seen as important partners of these businesses, such partnerships are valued only up to a point and are typically pre-defined by the business, through the provision of good service but in a regimented, highly disciplining fashion.

### 4.2.1   Innovative systems of service recovery and complaint management

Service recovery and complaint management are two key areas of modern marketing practice. They also represent distinct opportunities for businesses to demonstrate that they are truly customer centric. Such assertions are informed by above-mentioned fundamental assumptions that even the best type of service provision can occasionally fail and that companies need to act swiftly in order to rectify mistakes. Customer-compliance practices in these two areas, though, are highly unusual and are most adequately summarised in terms of the application of clear and rigid rules which complaining customers must follow and which are standard, standardised and are applied to all customers, irrespective of their demographic characteristics and of the length and type of their relationship with the provider. We should make our thinking clear by noting such standardisation of service recovery and complaint management as well as the adoption of a 'take it or leave it' attitude on the part of customer-compliance businesses should not be viewed as examples of poor or non-existent service recovery and complaint management. These companies have more than adequate returns systems. However, service recovery and complaint management are offered at a low, realistic cost, in order to keep their overall costs low, and subsequently pass on some of these cost savings to those customers whom we refer to as 'non-complainers' – customers who are rewarded for not adding to company cost structures by consistently calling and complaining about faulty products and services.[29]

# Case in Point – John's PC narrative

Various stories that we have collected during our decade-long research programme on customer-provider interactions across service provision contexts illustrate some of the issues that we as consumers face when attempting to communicate with customer-compliance companies. John was one such customer whom we interviewed a few years ago. At the time of the interview, John was working for an IT company. He had bought two computers from a trade outlet, and one of the machines had collapsed shortly after the purchase, following '*a lot of mysterious crashes*'. Prolonged negotiations with the company had achieved little. Although the hard disk drive was eventually replaced, the computer still randomly rebooted itself or crashed when in operation. After eight months of crashes and of the company claiming that it was John's fault and '*definitely a software problem*', John took on the task of persuading customer support to provide a solution to the recurring problems which had made the machine unusable. Following a series of lengthy telephone calls which tested John's negotiation and persuasion skills, the company agreed to inspect and possibly rebuild the machine. John shipped the computer but heard nothing from them. During a telephone call, John was told that the company could not provide information on the machine repair progress as they '*ship out about 200 machines a day and they'll have to check them manually. So, as soon as they know something, they'll go back to me. And stop ringing ... stop ringing 'em up*'. Episodes of verbal confrontation were repeated during later phone calls. What seemed to bother John most were what he referred to as routines and standard procedures that customers like him had to follow when complaining and the fact that during each separate interaction with the company, he had to retell his story, in detail, after having followed lengthy instructions:

> *Originally when you call up, you'd be put through to customer support. Customer support would then get a description of your problem, and they would either put you on a hold until a ... support technician was available or else they would get, if none were available they would say they'd 'get one to ring you back'.*

During each telephone interaction

> *customer support were asking a lot of 'Well, have you done this, have you checked that? Is this turned on, is that turned on?' sort of stuff I would have checked myself. ... But they had a set routine of questions they have to go all through and I, every time I rang up, they had to go through these ten-fifteen questions. ... I'm normally quite patient with them. But when they got to the stage where they were asking me questions I'd already answered, I was just at the stage where ... 'Sorry, don't wanna talk to you anymore. Put me on to somebody who knows what they're talking about.' ... each time I would call, I would explain all the history behind it and say ... 'I got this far last time, now I want to speak to somebody higher.'*

Company staff repeatedly refused to escalate the problem:

> *And ... they would just go 'No, sorry. We can't put you through to a manager until we identify your problem.' 'I'm sure if you turn around to anybody sitting next to you, they already know about my problem. So, put me through to a manager.' ... They seem to be ... stuck, they seem to have a sheet in front of them and they read out the questions. And that's all they know how to do.*

The empirical analysis about customer experiences such as John's raised an intriguing issue – some customers appeared to be 'disciplined' during inter-actions with their service providers, whereby the customer's behaviour is being channelled in a way which may be perceived as dissatisfactory by the consumer but which appears to suit the provider.

John's **Case in Point** was one of the first instances of customer compliance that we collected, empirically confirming some of our earliest expectations that certain businesses may intentionally deviate from expectations about service provision that one finds in many currently dominant marketing texts.[30] The case demonstrates how, contrary to literature expectations that communication during complaint interactions tends to be non-standardised (and that it should not be standardised),[31] customer-compliance businesses such as the one with which John was involved at the time of our inter-view with him meticulously design and control interactions with calling and complaining customers, partly by pre-defining the structure and parameters of such interactions, as John's narrative illustrates. John's interactions with the company were invariably and highly standardised. They can hardly be described as individualised, as marketers have been trained to expect and practise.

However, John's story goes even further, by illustrating how callers whom the company's IT database systems recognise as 'difficult' (serial complain-ers who have called the company before, possibly on a number of occasions, reporting faults or consistently complaining about a specific service failure) are often disciplined from the very start of the communication with front-line personnel. Such standardised communication is a particularly refined instrument of controlling customers; it rests on the use of regulated and rehearsed phrases such as 'This conversation will be recorded for training purposes only'. Such a phrase reminds 'trouble makers' such as John that the company's IT systems have recognised them, that a history of their previous calls and grievances is kept on record, that the company is fully knowledge-able of their past behaviour and 'complications' they have caused, and that the current call to the company will be observed, recorded, stored and added to the data and may be shared with other providers that may decide not to deal with the customer.

By meticulously designing the most mundane aspects of their interac-tions with complaining customers, especially with serial complainers such as John, customer-compliance businesses ensure that even determined complainers and aggressive callers will be effectively 'neutralised' and that their calls will most probably not escalate. Resolute complainers are thus not allowed to penetrate the skin of the organisation and their interactions are often only with front-line, typically outsourced, call-centre personnel. This is how customer-compliance businesses aim to first scrutinise and then if necessary restrain the minority of complainers who are known to customer-compliance companies and who substantially add to the cost of their service provision.

## Case in Point – Contact Details of CCBMs

Amazon, Ryanair and other customer compliance businesses exemplify the manner in which they design complaint channels for disgruntled customers wishing to lodge a complaint so as to restrict access and thus minimise contact points with financially and emotionally expensive callers. We visited a number of websites, expecting, as marketing theory teaches, it would be relatively easy to locate contact details, call centre and customer services information. Typically, the 'greeting' pages of these companies are replete with individualised service offerings, recommendations and similar customers' ratings. Noticeable across websites is the absence of clear and prominent indications of what customers should do if they are unhappy about some aspect of service provision and wish to inform the company about their experience.

It is not uncommon, as in the case of Amazon, for customers scrolling down the home page to eventually notice, at the very bottom of the page and in particularly small print, a set of four 'Let Us Help You' options. However, it is only one of these options that redirects customers to 'Returns'. Once having clicked the option, the customer is taken to yet another page with a 'Contact Us' button which, though highlighted, is not particularly prominent and is positioned towards the bottom of the page. A customer, who after having searched the website for contact details and is possibly both annoyed and exasperated at this point, may now be hopeful that Amazon's website will provide an email address or the telephone number of the customer services section of the company. However, clicking on the 'Contact us' button redirects the customer to another page, where they need to sign in before being 'allowed' to proceed and contact the service provider. Those customers who have still not given up the quest for justice or their search for revenge are eventually taken to a screen which lists their current orders and provides an option to contact the company by email and, allegedly, by telephone. Those customers who may prefer to talk to a company representative are redirected to a screen reproduced below which does not provide a local (in our case, a UK) number but offers the customer a 'Call Me Service' whereby they are forced to type in their own contact details, in the hope that the company will eventually respond by calling them. By the time we populated the webpage areas reproduced above, the best part of 20 minutes had been spent trying to figure out how and where to locate the 'contact details' of the company and its call centre (assuming that one existed), in the process of doing so navigating through a number of pages.

A typical scenario is illustrated below based on the website design of a number of CCBMs visited by the authors.

**Home page**
- Scroll to the bottom of the page where there are three columns. In the last one titled 'How can we help you' under which there are five options including 'how to make returns' and the last one which is 'Help'
- Click help and you arrive at the help page

**Help page**
- This page offers a number of links to all sorts of self-help systems but without a telephone number discernible.
- On the right hand side is a radio button which says contact us. Clicking on this brings you to an e-mail contact page with the company.
- Under the heading 'Most customers want to know', the last of 12 items contains the word 'More....'. Click here and you arrive at another page.

**Frequently asked questions**
- The site attempts once again to get the customer to use the self-help information but on the right hand side is a button labelled exactly the same as the button on the help page that previously led to the contact us e-mail. Clicking on it reveals a questionnaire and a list of your latest purchases.
- At the bottom is a row of buttons under 'How would you like to contact us', the middle button says 'Phone - call us'
- Clicking this button this brings you to another page.

**Questionnaire**
- You thought you were there but no - before they give the telephone number, they ask you to complete the 'short' questionnaire.
- Having completed the questionnaire above, the 'call us' is no longer greyed out and another window opens.

**Customer service**
- The information about which you are concerned appreas but yet no telephone number - they offer to call you either immediately or at some time in the future.
- At the very bottom of the page in faint blue text is their telephone number.

Complaining customers cost companies a lot of money because many of them expect personalised service, including from call-centre staff of CCBMs. Customised service requires personnel to be employed in an unproductive area of operations which generates no income. Individualised and attentive service recovery indeed costs companies such as CCBMs and thus reduces average transaction profitability. In fact, financially profitable customers, including non-complainers, often know their way around websites and require no support. Websites of CCBMs are therefore designed to discourage complaining. As the above diagram demonstrates, they have become major tools in the armoury of compliance businesses in their quest to reduce the average cost of transactions with customers.

The **Case in Point** provides an example of how customer compliance businesses closely regulate and shape interactions with customers, including online interactions, partly by maximising the effort that complainers or potential complainers need to invest in order to lodge their complaint or contact the customer services representatives of the company. The steps which disgruntled customers have to follow before contacting Amazon. com ensure that customers' perceptions of effort when attempting to complain are maximised[32] – contradicting the subjects of effort and perception of effort in marketing.[33] Current marketing thought advises providers to minimise effort and customers' perceptions of effort during complaining, in order to facilitate complaining as a form of feedback and intelligence gathering, and thus encourage complaints. However, the two preceding **Cases in Point** – those of John's narrative and Amazon's contact details – illustrate conscious planning on the part of businesses that aim to maximise complaint effort and, therefore, perceptions of effort on the part of customers, in order to deter complaining customers and especially serial complainers from repeatedly contacting the company and thus adding to its customer services costs.

Normative thinking is predicated on assumptions of complaints being legitimate until proven otherwise.[34] Customer compliance businesses seem to have reversed this principle of service recovery and complaint management. The above-noted legitimacy assumption in the literature is abandoned – a finding which is rarely documented even in the practitioner literature[35] and one that is absent in academic texts. Nonetheless, our empirical research demonstrates that making customers compliant invariably demands that customers' complaints, and especially those lodged by serial complainers, are treated as illegitimate by default. John and others are forced to persuade the provider that their complaints are worth investigating and should be resolved.

In order to fully appreciate such an argument, one should review reports in the practitioner press of 'issues' that some customers face when dealing with service providers. Largely due to the growth in the number and variety of communication outlets and vehicles available to dissatisfied customers, the 'democratised' public space, and the alleged 'empowerment' of customers, complaining has become a more prominent phenomenon. In 2006, UK's National Complaints Culture Survey (NCCS) reported a sharp rise in the number of complaints and the alleged widespread failure of providers to resolve them. Once again, in the practitioner literature, Croft[36] has attempted to account for a 'surge in complaints' against UK high street banks and the 'enormous' 'scale of complaining'. Lester[37] has analysed some 'personal horror stories' of customers, with problems supposedly 'getting worse'. The academic literature has been relatively slow to try and make sense of these developments, apart from branding such practices as unethical and unacceptable. Whereas the practitioner literature and the occasional academic writing view these company procedures as problematic, we treat at least some of them as ingredients of a planned and deliberate system of service provision and customer management that some companies have implemented in order to provide good service at low cost to the majority of their customers, while disciplining and – if necessary – ignoring, avoiding and 'expelling' customers who are perceived as standing in the way of the business achieving its financial aims.

---

### Section summary for managers:

o *Service provision as part of customer compliance is generally satisfactory and of good standard. It is marked by simplicity of ordering, speedy delivery, timeliness and secure payment systems.*

o *Customer compliance practices differ fundamentally from traditional service recovery in that companies practising compliance enforce rigid, standardised rules which are applied to all customers irrespective of their demographics and the length of their relationship with the company.*

o *Such compliance practices aim to reduce costs of service provision for providers, though some savings are passed on to their customers.*

---

### 4.2.2   The role of front-line personnel

Marketing academic analyses tend to over-emphasise the role and importance of stakeholder groups such as customers and business partners, while sidelining the study of employees and front-line employees in particular. Bowen and Johnston's[38] is a relatively early comment on the rarity of research on internal service recovery. To this day, the perceptions, attitudes and behaviours of employees as allegedly companies' 'internal customers' remain under-researched and largely less well understood and unexplained. A few years ago, Bell and Luddington[39] noted the scarcity of accounts of how customers' complaints affect employees. Although front-line staff have been officially pronounced as an important group in relationship marketing discourses, these 'internal customers' remain understudied and unappreciated. Marketers have written on, explained and learnt to effectively manipulate and shape customers' satisfaction, attitudes and behaviours; however, there is a pronounced absence of a more thorough comprehension of the nature and availability of support mechanisms for staff, of the 'psychological contract' with staff, and of staff recovery following customers' complaints.[40]

Managing employees and front-line staff is key to the service provision efforts of customer compliance businesses, necessitating a proper understanding of the role that they have been assigned in customer compliance systems and processes. Customer compliance businesses rely on these employees to actually implement compliance, whereby staff exact behaviour from customers which is deemed acceptable by the company. It is also front-line staff who carry out the channelling and standardisation of processes and interactions with customers. Consequently, such businesses seek to employ personnel who, when given authority by the computerised systems and regimented policies and standard operating procedures, can effectively carry out company expectations by handling equally well the compliant and the more resolute and vocal complainers. Staff have been shown to manage stress while also screening off abusive and potentially problematic customers such as those in Briner's[41] description of a rude customer interacting with a call-centre operative, with the operative threatening to 'put a note on his records' about the customer's rude behaviour. Such front-line employee reactions remind readers of Bolton and Houlihan's[42] discussion of the 'victimisation' of frustrated customers who are forced to comply with automated, mechanised and impersonal service. As will be shown next, while Bolton and Houlihan's analysis is of interest to this book, we do not view such customer compliance strategies and tactics as examples of 'victimisation' but are inclined to describe academic analyses reaching such conclusions as largely misguided, by failing to appreciate the strategic logic behind specific company actions, processes and policies.

## Case in Point – easyJet and the *Airline* programme

*Airline* is a UK documentary, also released in the US, which is a docu-soap presenting the stories of passengers and ground staff of the no-frills airline easyJet at Liverpool, Luton, Stansted and other UK airports. The programme enjoyed considerable popularity and has had a following in the UK since 1998, having been aired on UK's ITV, ITV2 and Sky TV channels. The programme has offered numerous examples to its viewers of the ways in which customer compliance businesses such as easyJet employ staff in order to manage their customers effectively. Episode 9 in Series 8 (2004), for instance, presents the story of a UK couple travelling to Alicante who miss their flight due to an alleged transfer to the wrong desk at the airport terminal. The easyJet staff member deals resolutely with the visibly anxious and distressed female passenger, offering on two separate occasions to transfer the couple to the next day's flight.

This offer is declined by the male passenger who becomes aggressive and shouts repeatedly at the easyJet representative, to which the representative responds by noting that the TV screens throughout the airport provide adequate information about check-in desks and departure gates to assist travelling passengers. In spite of the male customer's foul language and verbal abuse, drawing other passengers' attention to himself and the conversation, the staff member does not relent but repeatedly excludes him from the argument by raising her voice when responding to him and by focusing instead on the female passenger, while showing no visible signs of apprehension or agitation.

Following this exchange, the female passenger turns towards the camera, exclaiming that she and her partner had missed the check-in closure by a second only, to which the staff member responds that the length of the delay is not of consequence on this occasion – suggesting that what matters is following rules.

The scene ends with the staff member refusing to give in to the male passenger's demands and aggression but noting that the male passenger would not achieve anything and would most certainly not be allowed on board, no matter how much he shouts. The female passenger gives up at this point and both she and her partner leave the desk.

Far from relying solely upon hiring and promoting staff who are outgoing and confident during interactions with customers, as demonstrated in the easyJet **Case in Point**, customer compliance businesses tend to provide adequate training for staff in order to help them carry out their crucial role as the front-line enforcers of compliance mechanisms and regulations – empirically demonstrated during two separate pieces of empirical research carried out and documented by us in past publications. As demonstrated with respect to the difficulty that customers experience when attempting to lodge a complaint with such businesses and the absence of easily identifiable and readily available contact details, customer compliance businesses plan their procedures of dealing with customers in such a manner so as to minimise the direct, face-to-face or telephone contact with personnel. New technologies including voice recognition software and fully automated online interactions help avoid direct interactions altogether. Where possible, opportunities for face-to-face exchanges with abusive customers and complainers who are difficult to handle, as seen in the easyJet **Case in Point**, are reduced or, when and if possible, eliminated altogether.

However, apart from designing systems of automated interactions with customers, enforcing standard operating procedures (SOPs) which assist staff in their daily exchanges, and training staff to handle customers effectively, little additional support seems to exist for those employees who prove incapable of coping with the stress of customer compliance workplaces. Our empirical research at a number of call centres provided adequate evidence that front-line employees, such as the call-centre operatives working for customer compliance businesses, are expected to demonstrate an ability to handle stress when communicating with complainers. Employees follow strict procedures which are designed to safeguard the rest of the business from lengthy, emotionally exhausting and therefore economically unprofitable exchanges. Internal service recovery is typically minimal, if available at all. The rule when hiring staff – a rule of which staff are constantly reminded in such work environments – is '*swim or drown*', in the words of one of our interviewees. This description is rather similar to Bowen and Johnston's[43] argument that managers have 'little sympathy' for the effect that customer complaints may have on staff. Managers tend to view staff as being trained to 'cope with such situations'.

The work environment that we have depicted is far from calm; however, staff do appear empowered. Such an assertion invalidates certain academic expectations of the powerlessness of front-line employees who are forced to merely follow 'scripted rules'.[44] We agree that, as the easyJet **Case in Point** demonstrates, customer compliance businesses do not typically expect or even tolerate deviation on the part of their staff from the clear procedural scripts with which they are provided; nor does the management of customer compliance businesses favour initiative taking on the part of staff, for instance by accommodating the needs of habitual and serial or aggressive complainers. However, by relinquishing control, staff are paradoxically empowered – a description which does not fit accounts of 'a traditional command and control environment'.[45] Rather, relinquishing control which is associated with following strict and regimented SOPs (Standard Operating Procedures) appears to be non-problematic for staff. Front-line employees such as the earlier mentioned staff member in the *Airline* episode tend to internalise the dominant 'take it or leave it' discourse of customer compliance businesses. This turns employees, along with the businesses' customers, into subjects of governmentality, with employees adopting the culture and philosophy of service provision and especially the dictum that service recovery and complaint management procedures are designed and enforced by management and are not to be questioned. It is in this manner that employees turn into self-regulated actors – the price that they pay for working in an environment where rules designed by someone much higher in the corporate hierarchy force customers to submit and adopt a passive role during interactions. However, the employees' position – unlike that of the customers – is not weakened, as will be demonstrated next. Interviews carried out by the authors with front-line employees across such businesses demonstrate that many of them view such customer compliance procedures as beneficial to the company and, interestingly, to themselves. By placing the locus of control and responsibility for customer compliance procedures with an anonymous entity, 'the company' or 'management', employees are exonerated and made unaccountable for specific decisions while 'conditioned' customers come to know and accept that they should not 'fight the system'.

---

### Section summary for managers:

o *Customer compliance businesses rely on front-line staff to implement their compliance policies, procedures and systems.*
o *Employees are trained to understand and use compliance policies, including online systems which are easily and sometimes automatically updated.*
o *Compliance systems tend to empower employees who deal with difficult, abusive and emotionally demanding customers on a daily basis, knowing that management would not overrule their decisions.*
o *Customer compliance businesses resist attempts on the part of complainers to escalate complaints, and educate their customers that decisions made by front-line staff are not usually overruled.*
o *Customer compliance businesses tend to openly inform customers and the general public of their compliance policies, thus 'educating' existing and potential customers.*

---

### 4.2.3 Are customers truly empowered?

The marketing literature is replete with arguments about empowered customers, both in offline and online environments.[46] Even studies which do not explicitly address such issues reveal strong underlying assumptions about the increased power of service users. Prahalad and Ramaswamy[47] have been among the most influential and ardent supporters of a view of empowered consumers having more choices these days, in an alleged distinction from passivity of their offline predecessors. In the past, customers were a key yet external resource to providers, and they remained on the fringes, or outside, of value creation processes.[48] The current consensus in marketing circles is that customers are actively engaged with, and incorporated in, value creation activities, through embedded exchanges and personalised experiences with providers. Such assumptions and conclusions can be traced to Dabholkar's[49] claim that control and enjoyment are key to customers' evaluation of service encounters, especially when they involve some sort of automation. These ideas have gained momentum. Singh and Singh[50] argue that blogs 'radically alter the marketplace' as part of their discussion of the 'growing' 'power of Weblogs'. Customers' participation in and contribution to retailers' productivity, as part of a growing trend towards self-service, has been investigated.[51] To Balsamo,[52] the Internet has given birth to a new type of individual agency. Far from aiming to offer a representative review of this literature, we only note some additional recent contributions, including Harrison, Waite and Hunter's[53] discussion of new technology, information and empowerment of customers through information availability and increased choice – echoing earlier suggestions that control and choice affect customers' perceptions of ownership of choices. This belief in the empowering potential of virtual markets, with consumers overcoming information asymmetries and 'banding together' against providers, informs the thinking of Rezabakhsh et al.[54]

A comprehensive list of drivers behind this alleged customer empowerment is available in Doyle's (2006) practitioner piece on 'The evolution of self-service environments'. Self-service environments, it is suggested, have gained momentum and popularity in the five years preceding the publication of the article in question. They are found across sectors, have grown in sophistication and have reached a stage of development where they have turned into 'rich functional environments' allowing customers to fully interact with their providers. In such environments, customers enjoy 'significant control' and aspects of empowerment include 'choice of channel', 'choice of when', 'choice over type of interaction', 'choice over nature of interaction', 'increased comfort', 'increased confidence' and 'wider availability' – reminiscent of earlier pronouncements such as Shipman's[55] conclusion about the radical power shift and 'new consumer sovereignty' brought about by the Internet. To Murphy,[56] these developments mark 'the greatest transition of power in history', with consumers gaining power at the expenses of 'the mightiest corporations'.

The thesis of empowered customers can be linked to the earlier mentioned, equally dominant marketing and relationship marketing concepts as well as fashionable marketing theories such as the service-dominant logic.[57] The latter is often described as the highest achievement of customer-centric marketing and is viewed as a shift in orientation towards interactional approaches between customers and providers, where customers are valued as partners and collaborators and are approached as 'operant resources' in the marketing process.[58] Customer experience is inextricably linked with co-creation[59] – a concept which is not new and which has most certainly informed marketing thinking long before the service-dominant logic came to prominence,[60] but has gained currency in a climate espousing interdependence, dialogue, value and experience co-creation.[61]

Although representing a minority in marketing thought, some academics have questioned the rhetoric of customer empowerment. Barrutia and Echebarria,[62] for instance, remind us that there is a lack of consensus about drivers of empowerment. To Pires, Stanton and Rita,[63] the empowering effect of the Internet may have been unintended, while Harrison, Waite and Hunter[64] are even more critical in their conclusion that, in spite of the attractiveness of this rhetoric, consumers do not really feel empowered. In the context of financial service provision studied by them, consumers feel that the Internet may have empowered some; however, the sense of personal empowerment on the part of individual consumers has not been fully realised. Not being immediately relevant to the study of online interactions and the power balance between consumers and providers, Shankar, Cherrier and Canniford's (2006) 'Foucauldian interpretation' of 'consumer empowerment' raises similar doubts about customer empowerment. The authors question the very idea that having more choice benefits customers, and maintain that consumers may never be able to escape the operation of power that one finds in the marketplace. The literature on the shift of power from producers to consumers is duly questioned and much of what it offers is challenged, in particular its neoliberal assumptions.

Even more critical of standard assumptions of the liberating properties and consequences of new technologies is a recent study by Bonsu and Darmody,[65] where customers are described as 'genuinely empowered' but also 'entrapped' when implicated in the production processes of providers. Bonsu and Darmody's study of the co-production processes and philosophy of the online game Second Life concludes that 'co-creation is a veneer of consumer empowerment in a world where market power, in large measure, still resides in capital'.[66] Empowerment through co-creation may be nothing more than a strategic tool for companies to 'revitalize the firm's capitalist zeal and market control'[67] while not enhancing considerably the customers' experiences but saving corporate resources and 'transferring responsibilities' for 'costly productive activities'. It is in Zwick and Dholakia's[68] as well as Zwick, Bonsu and Darmody's[69] analyses that one finds additional challenges to assumptions of customers gaining control. What one observes is not necessarily increased customer power but reduced privacy, the availability of perfected data on customers, and the rendering of customers 'fully transparent' and accessible by marketers – something that would not have been achievable with offline technology. Furthermore, there is an increased tendency for consumers' online identities to be actively constructed by businesses – an idea borrowed from Sotto[70] and interpreted by Zwick and Dholakia as a sign of marketers still being in control of interactions with consumers, with data on individual customers now practically becoming and constituting the customer's identity.

## Case in Point – Empowerment the Amazon way

Humphreys'[71] account offers an intriguing insight into the relationships that Amazon nurtures with its customers and the effect that they have on customer empowerment. A number of practices are identified which empower those registered on the company's website but which also act as examples of 'surveillance' of customers on the part of the company. What Humphreys means by 'surveillance' and 'individuation' is the ability of companies, through modern technologies, to constitute customers as objects of knowledge, whereby marketers use technology to study customers, obtain knowledge about them and apply such knowledge in order to 'classify' and 'separate' customers. Examples of three of Amazon's more prominent practices illustrate this fine balancing of empowerment and disempowerment. For instance, there is Amazon's 'wish list' – a list of the items referred to and checked by the customer. This 'wish list' helps configure the individual customer into a 'case study' of 'purchases and desires', leaving the customer with nothing to classify.[72] Ultimately, Amazon creates such 'case studies' and collates them into segments, offering products that have been bought by someone else belonging to the segment ('niche'). The second practice is that of suggesting to customers 'what you might enjoy' items which help 'manage' consumer desires. Amazon has also been among the first companies that we refer to as customer compliance businesses to invite its customers to actively contribute content such as reviews, guides and lists, with some customers becoming 'top reviewers'. Customers apparently enjoy watching and assessing other customers' choices and, in turn, take pleasure in being watched – a peculiarity which Humphreys labels 'voyeuristic', sharing similarities with Amazon's Listmania! service as an example of the pervasive surveillance of the individual on such websites.

As the preceding discussion demonstrates, by utilising new Internet, intranet and call-centre technologies, marketers have come to identify, design and apply techniques and tactics not only to empower but also control customers. Customer compliance businesses seem to simultaneously empower and disempower, constrict and regulate the behaviour of their customers. However, this is implemented differently from traditional control, as documented in some marketing accounts. Customers may indeed appear empowered when they are allowed to customise the service offers of customer compliance providers. Nonetheless, when they wish to express their dissatisfaction, in the case of service failure, consumer agency is minimised or eliminated altogether. Individual action and initiative taking is successfully resisted by such businesses. By pre-setting the parameters and options of interactions with customers (prior to the complaint interaction), by extensively using SOPs and making frequent references to such 'company procedures' (as a reminder of who really is in charge), by increasing customers' effort when attempting to communicate and negotiate with the provider, and by increasing the visibility of the customer's low level of control over the entire process (for instance, by resorting to the earlier mentioned standard phrases during interactions), customer compliance businesses actively disempower a minority of customers.

Initiative taking and resistance to customer compliance procedures and policies are rarely successful when they are planned and carried out by individual customers. Collective action such as group litigation or lobbying may be more effective if a case becomes particularly visible, thus possibly temporarily turning the table in favour of the customer. However, examples of the latter are rare. In fact, there are only a few instances when customer compliance businesses have relented under collective pressure or the demands of bodies with legitimate authority such as local councils, regulatory authorities and even regional and national governments. Ryanair's history of interactions with such bodies provides strong support for our thinking. Marketing scholars may want us to think that that there is a clear distinction between individual and collective influence,[73] that 'collective opposition to injustice' is necessary[74] and can affect underlying institutional conditions.[75] However, there is little evidence in support of such claims as far as customer compliance businesses are concerned. Many customers have received dismissive letters from such businesses. **Case in Point: British Airways' customer relations** is an example of such correspondence following the 2010 industrial dispute in the company which caused considerable traffic disruption and flight cancellations. Note the unwillingness of the company to even recognise, let alone address, the customers' dissatisfaction. Nor are any compensation or reimbursement offered.

## Case in Point – Customer relations

Below is the actual wording of an e-mail received from a major legacy airline following disruptions to their schedule due to a strike of cabin staff in 2010. The tone, wording and content of the e-mail offer no concessions to the customer's concerns. It is likely to have been standardised wording sent to all complaining customers.

**From:** <airline> Customer Relations
**Sent:** 19 July 2010 13:47
**To:** <Customer e-mail address>
**Subject:** Your Response from <airline> Customer Relations
Dear <Customer name>

I apologise for the delay in replying to you. I can understand why you are so disappointed to pay a cancellation fee for your flight. Please accept my sincere apologies.

It became increasingly difficult for us to absorb the extra administration costs and other overheads when people book and then cancel, and we now have no choice but to pass some of this on.

Many of our policies are based on comments we have previously received from our customers. We know expectations continuously change though, and this is why your feedback is so important to us. We have a manager responsible for our ticket cancellation policy. I have passed your comments to them. They will look at all the feedback we have received from you and will use it to help them improve the policy in future.

Thank you for taking the time to let me know and for giving me the opportunity to respond to your concerns. We look forward to welcoming you on board soon.

Best regards

<Customer relations operative name>

Customer Relations

Practices as those presented in the two **Cases in Point** in this section can hardly be labelled as customer empowering. Customer attempts to escalate their individual requests and concerns are usually blocked. Even when escalated, they rarely achieve much, since the companies practising customer compliance appear to be largely immune from negative publicity. Even collective action on the part of disgruntled customers may prove to be ineffective, in spite of negative media coverage, word of mouth and legal challenges – as will be shown in the discussion on media coverage and reaction to customer compliance practices. It is a fact that even during the current recession, many customer compliance businesses continue to grow and attract the custom of large sections of the population across developed economies. Readers are regularly reminded of the UK public's alleged falling out of love with IKEA,[76] about dissatisfaction with the unfriendliness of IKEA staff and fights over special offers at store opening.[77] However, even such highly visible reports on these companies, in the press and in consumer-watchdog programmes such as a BBC Newsnight programme dedicated to Ryanair seem to achieve little. The profitability of customer compliance businesses remains intact, and injuries caused by negative viral marketing and aggressive blogs such as 'I hate IKEA'[78] and 'IKEAAttack'[79] are equally minimal.

Very recently, articles have appeared, mostly in the business press, of customer compliance businesses actually impeding the actions of complainers or even spying on troublesome customers – yet another form of control that we have uncovered in the process of researching the practices of these businesses. *The Guardian*,[80] for instance published an analysis piece on IKEA facing a judicial investigation in France following allegations that it had paid private detectives to snoop on workers and investigate the private lives of disgruntled customers who had complained about IKEA product quality and service lead times. The press commented that these type of surveillance practices – attempting an extreme compliance – contrasted with the friendly face of affordable furnishing which the company has been trying to promote. Accusations were made that the company had tried to access a range of personal data, including criminal records and confidential details of any dealings with the justice system on the part of the disgruntled customers in question. In a statement, IKEA stated that all media reports would be taken 'extremely seriously' and that the company would fully co-operate with the state prosecutor's investigation. IKEA also reiterated that the company's ethical rules were very clear and that it aimed to operate with honesty and transparency in all host markets. IKEA's statement also claimed that respect for people's private lives was among the most strongly held values of the group and that the company strongly disapproved of any practice which called that value into question. Three staff members were placed on leave of absence pending the enquiry. The company has not commented further on this matter, as the enquiry is still underway. However, if it is found guilty, IKEA's practices will demonstrate yet another example of compliance and control through data management and surveillance on the part of a company that is generally considered to be among the most customer-centric organisations in its industry.

In summary, we reiterate that customer sovereignty is limited and pre-defined by customer compliance businesses. Many of the practices documented in this book clearly have both empowering and disempowering properties and effects; however, the disempowering consequence is more pronounced – first, by observing their customers, collecting data on them and designing their virtual identities independently from customers and often without their consent, and second, by harnessing such data to control and govern customers, various consumption-related aspects of their experiences are controlled by the company.

The control that customer compliance businesses seek and often achieve is not an entirely new phenomenon in marketing practice. Many companies which cannot be labelled customer compliance businesses have long used data and database management to manage, shape, and mould customers. More generally, the assertion that marketing has constricting and controlling properties[81] is not new. However, customer compliance businesses have

---

### Section summary for managers:

o *Marketing literature suggests customers are empowered – they have more choice these days and use web blogs, online reviews and personal recommendations to affect opinions, corporate reputations and consumption choices.*

o *Customer experience is frequently theorised with respect to co-creation – another driver of the alleged customer empowerment.*
o *Customer compliance practices question some of these arguments and conclusions, demonstrating, for instance, that greater choice (which is itself questionable) does not mean that customers can escape control in the marketplace which assumes different formats – one of these being compliance.*
o *Far from being universally empowered, customers may also be entrapped by businesses using new technologies.*

transformed the nature and outcomes of such control and have developed new, innovative ways of simultaneously empowering and subjugating customers.

### 4.2.4   Relations with customers, customer loyalty and branding

Much has been written about the development and maintenance of long-term relationships with customers and other stakeholders, yet the literatures of service provision and service recovery have failed to acknowledge sufficiently the role of relations during service recovery.[82] Some academics have argued that there is a need to develop further our understanding of the link between service recovery and the history of customer-provider exchanges.[83] Puga Leal and Pereira[84] call for additional research on the association between relationship duration and dissatisfied customers' responses to service failure. In spite of the absence of empirically confirmed knowledge on the subject, it is frequently assumed that relationships with one's customers are critical to customers' judgements about service provision and service recovery, as well as to customer satisfaction. Normative assumptions of customer loyalty affecting primary customer satisfaction, service recovery and post-complaint satisfaction abound. Service loyalty is often measured in terms of key service marketing constructs such as repeat purchase and customers' repatronage. The literature tends to distinguish among types of loyalty, based on ingredients such as attitudes and repatronage. Combined weak or absent relative attitudes and repeat patronage, for instance, suggest absence of loyalty. Latent loyalty is observed in situations of high positive attitudes, relative to those held for competing offers, and low repeat patronage. While the ingredients for forming and maintaining longer-term relationships are in place, constraints such as social norms and adherence to social expectations may limit the actual impact of loyalty on customers' actual buying behaviours. Low attitudes compared to those held for competitors' products and services may result from perceptions of low differentiation or high substitutability among product or service offers. When combined with high levels of repeat patronage, such attitudes mark a situation of spurious loyalty, where services may be consumed simply due to one's familiarity with the offer, social pressures, or the persuasion tactics of providers. The preferred option, to marketing academics and service marketing practitioners, is obviously that of high (and positive) relative attitudes and consistent high repatronage. Here one finds the pool of what are commonly referred to as 'loyal customers', who tend to influence positively general attitudes towards a service, product or a brand by recommending them to family members, friends and colleagues.

Marketing commentators working in the area of online marketing, e-marketing, digital marketing and e-commerce have recently supplemented, or complemented at times, the analysis of loyalty with that of risk and trust. Such discussions counter-balance earlier literature emphasis on benefits to consumers from online shopping and online interactions, with respect to choice, comparison, information availability, efficiency and convenience. Pavlou's[85] analysis is part of a growing tradition which describes digital environments as impersonal, distant and marked by non-direct interactions, generating safety and security concerns. Risk – defined as the belief in potential suffering, or perceptions of uncertainty and likely negative consequences[86] – is treated as inevitable in e-marketing and digital marketing practice. It relates to possible mismanagement of financial and personal data, with private and embarrassing personal data being disclosed or shared. Consumers are also wary of data loss, with privacy concerns covering issues as diverse as the preventive actions on the part of providers (behavioural uncertainty), quality and reliability of Internet infrastructures (environmental uncertainty). Customers tend to share perceptions of potential monetary loss when dealing with a vendor whom they have never seen and who may be geographically distant, with no interaction[87] and cues[88] available to customers in order to assess a-priori the vendor's reputation or intentions. Therefore, it should not be surprising that security and privacy concerns fundamentally affect online behavioural intentions and repatronage.

This pervasiveness of perceptions of risk in online and digital environments has brought to the fore discussions of trust in online transactions. To Stewart et al.,[89] trust is a subjective probability calculated by the consumer that the digital transaction will occur as expected, in accordance with the customer's prior expectations. Favourable perceptions of behavioural and environmental uncertainty negatively affect perceptions of risk and may even engender loyalty. There is little disagreement in the literature that such trust acts as a key antecedent of purchase intentions, across service contexts, service situations and cultural environments. Therefore, it should not be surprising that trust is actively nurtured by customer compliance businesses, and that different types of trust are used by these businesses to attract and retain customers. Trust, as designed and practised by customer compliance businesses, is an amalgam of credibility (i.e., sincerity attributed to one's partner) and benevolence (lack of motivation for harming one's partner). While trust is emphasised by such companies, building upon their reputation as reliable businesses, lesser importance is accorded to developing relationship-embedded equity with their customers. Loyalty to businesses practising customer compliance may be weaker or it could be behavioural only and not attitudinal – loyalty of the 'spurious' type described by us earlier. Customer compliance businesses know and understand their customers; they are aware of, and capitalise on, customers' pervasive search for bargains and the weakened link between customers and brands that several commentators have noticed.[90] Therefore, loyalty is not necessarily defined in terms of the strength of customers' identification and association with brands or service offers but with respect to customers' familiarity with providers and their confidence in the providers' offers. It seems that it is one's familiarity with an offer or a provider that becomes the critical consideration as far as repatronage in the context of customer compliance is concerned, for confidence in the security of online transactions with customer compliance businesses is paramount. Repeat interactions and the resulting familiarity with such providers, and not loyalty as such, matter to customers, thus reaffirming the centrality of perceptions of risk and security[91] or trustworthiness[92] to such service provision.

Had online environments been marked by lesser and fewer privacy and financial risks, loyalty may have remained as important to customer compliance businesses as it is to traditional, offline providers in the service contexts populated by this new breed of companies. However, in light of widespread and growing perceptions of risk,[93] customer compliance businesses capitalise on consumers' unwillingness to engage in remote purchases. By building their reputation as reliable and trusted providers, they become household names with proven track record of managing successfully customer relationships and customer data. Unlike some of their competitors, though, customer compliance businesses aim to affect customers' confidence in the abilities and morality of providers, with cognitive type of trust taking precedence over affective trust,[94] in line with our conviction of the lesser propensity of developing long-term loyalty and equity-based relations with such providers. Trusting behaviour is determined by its rational, not emotional, components[95] and is defined as firm-specific rather than general.

Our conclusion of a partial replacement of 'loyalty' with 'familiarity' and 'trust', as regards customer compliance businesses, challenges commonplace expectations about the ingredients of successful service provision and differentiation; however, it confirms Mitchell's[96] observation that consumers 'pre-select' providers in order to avoid risk, and Szymanski and Hise's[97] conclusion that service provision is marked not so much by expectations of relationship building but financial security. Even if 'relationships' exist between customer compliance businesses and their customers, they are economic and legal ties which remind readers more of the financial bonds discussed by Berry[98] than the long-term, mutually rewarding relationships based on equity, trust, communications and involvement described by Gummesson[99] or the symbiotic marketing and emotional intelligence emphasised by Osarenkhoe.[100] This lesser emphasis on relation-building may also be viewed as a natural company reaction to growing consumer scepticism,[101] cynicism,[102] and fickleness.

## *Chapter summary for managers:*

o *Customer compliance businesses have reversed power relations between customers and businesses.*

o *Such businesses capitalise on customers' increased search for bargains, offering lower cost services in return for a certain loss of freedom and self-determination on the part of customers.*

o *Relations that customers form with customer compliance businesses are not marked by loyalty but by perceptions of reduced risk. It seems that it is trust in customer compliance businesses, and not attitudinal loyalty towards them, that drives the competitiveness of these companies.*

o *Where loyalty towards customer compliance businesses exists, it is rational and behavioural, and not emotional.*

# 5  Automated Market and Marketing Research

**Key questions in this chapter:**

o *Does your company undertake formal market and marketing research?*
o *Do you integrate your call centres and websites in your company's market and marketing research efforts?*
o *Do you undertake data mining and practise automated marketing whereby data input by customers is used to automatically update pricing, stock control, placing orders with suppliers and generating real-time management reports?*

## 5.1  The old and new faces of market and marketing research

Market and marketing research have both undergone remarkable change during the last 50 years. Early thinking and practice in both areas were shaped by the arrival of the research surveys, and more specifically the mail surveys that guided marketers' advertising efforts. More recent additions to the intelligence gathering inventory include correlation analysis, experimentation, the advent of focus groups and motivation analysis, the establishment of research departments and specialised courses teaching these two subjects. Many current practices of research, data acquisition and analysis with which we are familiar appeared in the early to mid-twentieth century. Of interest to this discussion, though, is the boost that market and marketing research experienced following the earlier noted shift in marketing from the production concept to the marketing concept.[1] The boost that research experienced back then reflected a move from an internal focus in many companies to a position best described as externally oriented. Research was now viewed as key to decision-making – it linked business thinking with external developments.

New developments shook market and marketing research once again, in the 1980s and 1990s. Turbulent environments, the increased competition noted in earlier sections of this book, fast-shifting consumer tastes and fads have allegedly added pressures to practise customer centricity, reinforcing the lead role played by intelligence gathering across sectors and industry environments. Changes in market conditions altered commonly-held expectations about, as well as the very nature of, research. Additional discontinuity was introduced when markets entered, in the 1980s, the so-called PC technology era.[2] Unlike their predecessors, researchers and analysts could use personal computers to gather and analyse data quickly and more efficiently, and report their findings in real time. The work of analysts has been facilitated by the birth of a new set of data collection and analysis tools, including the computer assisted telephone interviewing and computer assisted personal interviewing, used by call-centre operatives.

In the mid-1990s, information technology continued to transform daily business. Although initially applied to accounting, IT rapidly affected sales, marketing and other business functions.[3] Analysts identified unexpected applications of research – database marketing, real-time market research and database mining, among others. In hindsight, we can clearly distinguish between the earlier, one-way platforms of research through communication and the more recent, interactive approaches that have affected operational and strategic management across sectors. These technologies were to provide customers with immediate access to companies while also allowing companies to be in direct contact with their customers. Service providers could instantly match customer needs with their propositions – increasingly achieved automatically with the assistance of back-office software.

The growing volume of online trade in the late 1990s and early 2000s provided companies with additional opportunities to collect, store, analyse and use data. It became a common practice for companies to use their websites to collect and process information – an increasingly essential ingredient of their e-marketing practices. Ever lower-cost electronic storage means that businesses can store large sets of data indefinitely, from which they can extract and use the information necessary to facilitate decision-making. The collective memory of customers can be retained, organised, managed, accessed and used relatively easily and cheaply. Massive amounts of data are also collected through new channels in both primary research (online surveys and online tracking) and secondary research (marketing databases, URLs, search engines, newsgroups and blogs). Research costs have been reduced, partly because customers themselves often provide the data used by companies – as noted earlier in our discussion – but also due to the reduced amount of paperwork that has to be handled and the length of time necessary to complete ordering and payment.[4] Reporting is real-time, analysis has been enabled by back-office software, interviewees can be carefully profiled through the system of assembling panels, and personalised reports fit specific, highly idiosyncratic research needs.

---

**Section summary for managers:**

o *While market and marketing research was traditionally an expensive endeavour, modern technologies have reduced research-related costs.*

o *Technologies have altered the nature, methods and uses of market and marketing research. Huge amounts and variety of data and knowledge can be stored and analysed at low cost, deriving rich and up-to-date understanding of customers' browsing and purchasing habits, without their knowledge.*

o *The growing volume of online and call-centre business has redesigned traditional supply chains, with customer compliance businesses interacting with and researching their customers directly.*

o *Successful customer compliance companies effectively collect and possess customer data, typically holding such data on one database or on a few, connected databases, thus reducing the costs and increasing the effectiveness of data mining for purposes of market and marketing research.*

---

## 5.2   The research practices of customer compliance businesses

The entrepreneurial businesses practising customer compliance extensively use database marketing and technological advancements to undertake research which is then used to make better decisions. It may be expected that such businesses would share some 'universal' research needs and practices of traditional companies, possibly explaining the scarcity of analysis on this subject. However, customer compliance businesses seem to have replaced traditional market and marketing research with new practices worthy of analysis and copying, as discussed next. All research innovations which are reviewed below have turned out to be of consequence to the overall strategic and competitive success of these companies. Among all innovations, real-time analysis, reduced human intervention, back-office software and database marketing appear to be particularly significant as well as promising in terms of providing opportunities for other businesses to benchmark against successful customer compliance research practices.

We have clustered the various research innovations in groups, revealing different traits of customer compliance businesses – discouraging complaints; research through database marketing; real-time e-marketing research; research through interactive and network marketing; and 'bare' market and marketing research. As regards the first ingredient, or aspect, of research (discouraging complaints), much of what has traditionally been written about market and marketing research assumes that interactions with dissatisfied customers and feedback obtained from them are valuable forms of research.[5] As noted previously, commentators such as Harari[6] have long supported ardently the view that complainers may be more valuable to companies than strategic planners, as the information and advice that they provide are free. Huppertz[7] too notes that complaints help management identify problems with service provision. Even with respect to some companies that we label customer compliance businesses, academics assume that research carried out by contacting dissatisfied customers is worth the effort and investment. Low-cost airlines, for instance, are advised to obtain feedback about their operations from dissatisfied customers. Typical is Zaid's[8] mentioning a study which concluded that complaints were an opportunity to improve customer service. Negative word of mouth, on the other hand, can severely and negatively affect business operations and profitability. The conclusion is that companies such as what we define here as customer compliance businesses should incorporate in-flight surveys. Similarly Heskett et al.[9] attribute the success of some airlines, which we view as customer compliance businesses, to careful examination of customer feedback and the design of novel feedback systems.

Contrary to common expectations about research, and as already discussed by us, the intelligence gathering and analysis value of complaints appears to be of relatively little use to customer compliance businesses.[10] Although the notion of carrying out research through complaint gathering and processing may be appealing, these companies tend to monitor sales online and instantly. They use extensive management information systems and online surveys, and purchase ready analyses at a fraction of the cost of dealing with complaining customers, many of whom are viewed as a nuisance rather than as a source of valuable information. Far from relying on complaints to uncover weaknesses and faults in service provision, customer compliance businesses can typically obtain information faster, more cheaply and more accurately through the analysis of real-time sales and reports on trends and comparative websites operating in most business areas where this new compliance model has been introduced. Some types of information are in fact freely available on the Internet about competitors' activities in areas of pricing and product feature decisions, special offers, and marketing communications.

Customer compliance businesses automate and simplify research by gathering valuable data from websites and knowledge repositories which report and assess analysis undertaken by research agencies. Surveys, including the 2004 survey on the airline industry reported by Doganis (2006), have proved useful to customer compliance businesses operating in this sector. Such research-related choices reflect the generally growing use of secondary data and ready reports when addressing marketing research problems, partly because of the wide availability of free or cheap data over the Internet from private-sector, public-sector and syndicated sources. Alternatively, companies tend to combine the data collected in their databases with customer transaction records and secondary data of the type described above. Computer-driven algorithms linking current demand to current price are also increasingly used as a form of research. Some low-cost airlines use algorithms to ensure high load factors and thus maximise profitability. Such techniques appear to be commonly employed by other customer compliance companies such as eBay and Amazon, and are widespread in the travel, tourism and leisure sectors.

Websites have adequate systems for tracking and amending orders and for returning goods. Importantly, though, there is often no telephone number provided to complain outside the standardised system available on the website, the earlier example of Amazon, providing an illustration of such practices. Where telephone numbers are made available on the company's website, the path of finding them is rather obscure – typically not on the home page, and, in the case of Amazon four clicks away from the home page. Websites may not be supported by call centres either, or may charge heavily for their use if they exist, thus deterring not only the escalation of complaints but also, at times, first-time complaints. Such practices remain misunderstood by some customers and academics alike; however, it will be demonstrated how many customers appear to have become compliant and appreciate such customer compliance systems.

Analysts typically associate the design and use of databases with the work undertaken by marketing research agencies; however, such databases form the foundation of the marketing research strategy of many customer compliance businesses. Our earlier mentioned research with call-centre staff has revealed that each contact with customers presents an opportunity for the provider to collect valuable up-to-date customer information. Examples include the provision of registration information, physical transactions with customers, telephone and online queries. Databases have turned into highly valuable assets containing information on past interactions, customers' choices and responses to company initiatives, customers' demographics (age, gender, income) and psychographics (interests, activities, opinions), with all entries providing extra knowledge about their target markets and needs.[11] To some customer compliance businesses at least, the information contained in databases about customer demographics, psychographics, behaviours and lifestyle may account for much of the value of the business and is therefore jealously guarded, since such information may assist the business in discovering[12] and satisfying[13] wants and demands, resolving issues of customer defection, and strengthening relationships with existing consumers. Marketing databases have thus turned into a key tool of intelligence gathering and strategic sense making.

The extensive use of databases and the associated introduction of loyalty cards has allowed companies like Tesco to 'stock up' 'inside knowledge' on consumers.[14] Customer compliance businesses can individually profile their customers, identify precisely their needs, and design marketing offers specifically targeted at them as individuals, thus also obviating the need for segmentation as traditionally practised. Similarly, banks, and especially the financial service providers that belong to the set of customer compliance businesses, hold so much data on individual customers,[15] following the amalgamation of many financial institutions into single holdings, that at least some of them can write direct mail letters to a small sample of customers and then program computers to profile the replies against thousands of individual pieces of information held on a single customer. The same direct mail letter can then be sent out to matching profiles, based on entries in the company database, producing typically a very high response rate and avoiding customer annoyance with 'junk mail' or 'spam' emails. Some customer compliance businesses in retail have adopted a similar strategy to carry out research and marketing operations based on the data contained in their extensive databases. They profile past customer purchases and program their computer systems to offer the same products to customers perceived by the database as 'similar'. It is worthwhile visiting Amazon.com to witness how the system offers 'Product B' to people who also bought 'Product A'. The company offers its customers 'Today's Recommendations for You', 'New for You', 'Coming Soon for You', and 'Customers Who Bought this Item also Bought...' categories. This IT-enabled system works effectively. Traditional retailers have always grouped products, but they cannot match customer profiles as efficiently as done by these database-driven customer compliance businesses. It is in this manner that database marketing provides a reliable foundation for the impersonal but highly effective dialogue of customer compliance businesses with their customers, through fast collection, storage and processing of necessary information on customers' traits, purchase patterns, preferences, past interactions and complaints with the provider.

Real-time e-marketing research is a relatively new development in research practice. It relies upon unique buyer-seller communications, immediate access to information, and freedom from the limits of traditional, linear, one-way messages to passive audiences.[16] Relations with customers are technology-mediated, with providers using electronic means to inform, persuade and promote products or services.[17] The objectives of e-marketing are not dissimilar from those of conventional marketing – to identify and satisfy needs. However, the means to achieve these objectives are rather distinct. For instance, both 'pure-click' businesses and 'brick and click' companies treat the company's website as a prime opportunity to attract customers and interact with them.[18] The website is a source of valuable data, data mining, and after-sales support[19] and is a medium of interacting with people, some of whom may be difficult to reach when using conventional research methods. However, websites are used differently and more actively by customer compliance businesses – to be expected, considering that some foundational e-commerce principles and e-commerce research principles were invented in the airline industry[20] and by some of the earliest and most successful customer compliance businesses. Ryanair, Southwest Airlines and easyJet embraced early the new technologies, in order to cut down costs. They started selling electronic tickets, innovated by using their websites for promotional purposes, and were among the first to encourage customers to access information online, to register their preferences and make purchases online. More than 95 per cent of Ryanair's business is being booked online.[21]

Various customer compliance businesses have come to rely heavily on their websites to collect information about customers, their preferences, level and sources of satisfaction, and consequences of dissatisfaction. easyJet applies the power of e-marketing for its promotional efforts, general communication with customers (including automated mobile phone text messaging) and information gathering. The company recently used the services of DREAMmail, in

2005, in order to email existing customers and find out which customers cared to open emails distributed by the airline. Advertising and other types of marketing communications are frequently implemented online, with the service provider carefully monitoring responses to their campaigns. Customers' reactions to frequent announcements about promotions on such websites – including visiting websites, browsing through specific sections, purchasing or non-purchasing of services – are a prime method of gathering information about them. easyJet's brand communications manager Andrew Berks argues that the company is in a good position to track the performance of its marketing campaigns, being assisted by e-marketing developments. It is a system that delivers the 'smartest conversion to bookings'.[22]

Interactive marketing refers to face-to-face, interpersonal interactions among individuals for mutual benefit, while network marketing has been traditionally used to describe relationships among businesses which assist the co-ordination of business activities.[23] With businesses expected to interact with one another's systems, physical resources and staff,[24] network marketing was primarily applied to the collaborative efforts in business to business marketing. However, interaction marketing and network marketing are increasingly being applied interchangeably and with reference to the relations that companies establish and develop with customers. Interaction marketing and network marketing, as practised by customer compliance businesses, rest primarily on round the clock website accessibility and use. Customers may re-visit the website at any time, to check for updated information and the latest offers of a customer compliance business. During these visits, they leave digital trails which allow companies to monitor carefully and record customer behaviours. For instance, easyJet uses WebTrends to observe directly and in real time customers' actions and, consequently, to make accurate inferences about their decision-making processes.[25] Such information is used to target customers individually and more effectively.

Although not practised by customer compliance businesses only, online tracking is an example of how novel research practices can contribute to the success and competitive advantage of some businesses. Through the use of cookies and ever more sophisticated databases containing thousands of pieces of information on hundreds of thousands of customers, company systems recognise individual customers even before they attempt to log into their accounts on company websites. Online tracking obviates the need for traditional-style segmentation, with the individual customer, and not the 'cluster' or set of customers, becoming the target. It also reduces the need for traditional experimentation,[26] for providers can carry out market and marketing research at a fraction of the cost of traditional experimentation by varying aspects of the marketing mix (such as the pricing, packaging features, communications such as sales promotions, discounts and special offers, service and warranty features, financing options, etc.) and observing online the reaction of individual customers as well as their audiences as a whole. Instantaneous 'feedback', in terms of behavioural responses of customers to changes in marketing mix ingredients manipulated by the provider, can be incorporated into swift alterations to packaging, services and experiences offered to customers in order to reflect current needs and fashions. These are not the delayed alterations which typically follow traditional, timely and costly research which relies on gathering, collating and assessing the perceptions of disgruntled customers and their self-reports on likely future intentions, rather than actual behaviours.

Online tracking is basically a low cost, highly efficient and effective type of observation. As such it combines cost effectiveness with all features of observation as a type of method of data collection which have turned it into such a prominent form of research in corporate ethnography but also elsewhere. Thus, rather than surveying or interviewing complainers (who provide the company with responses about their motivation, feelings, and attitudes and whose responses may be malicious, tendentious, insincere but may also be affected by memory effects, self-report problems and personal interpretation of the questions asked), through online observation such as online tracking, customer compliance businesses are able to watch what individual customers actually do, how they react to and interact with offers and products, through a process of systematic, accurate and objective recording of patterns of actual behaviours and occurrences. Importantly, online tracking is also a type of natural observation, and as such does not suffer from shortcomings of contrived and artificial experimentation and non-natural observation settings. It is also direct in nature, yet it is inconspicuous and can be highly structured, with the provider deciding when and how to manipulate various ingredients of its offers, in order to study customers' reactions.

There have been reports of some opposition on the part of customers to these new market and marketing research tools. For instance, Alreck and Settle[27] maintain that the 'public' is 'more opposed than hospitable' to such merchant practices. In spite of such accounts of alleged resistance, it seems neither active nor widespread. Alreck and Settle argue that empirical evidence can be presented of 'substantial reluctance' of customers to provide businesses such as the ones studied by us here with information which assists their automated research practices. We have also come across claims of the exploitation of consumers, of privacy nightmares and of serious breaches of ethical standards of behaviour on the part of companies practising online observation.[28] Nonetheless, as will be demonstrated in the penultimate chapter of this book, a substantial number of customers seem to readily provide customer compliance businesses with the data required in order to carry out the activities described above.

We visited easyJet's website recently, in order to experiment with its interactive and research facilities. When initially accessing the website, visitors are being asked to select their nationality and language by clicking the respective national flag icons. Once in the website, the visitor realises the degree to which it is dominated by advertising campaigns, promotions and additional information on product packages (offering flights, hotels, car hire and other 'auxiliary' services – a prime example of link or affiliate marketing). Clicking on any of these icons provides easyJet with real-time, reliable and objective data on the popularity of their latest offers and promotions, customers' reactions to their advertising campaigns and various service options (including the selection of specific flights, flexible fare options, purchase of 'additional' services, time and date of purchase of the service in advance of the travel date, or simply browsing through the website prior to the purchase). Additional but important information on the frequency of customer visits, their browsing and purchase history is easily collected, updated and analysed. This is largely due to the fact that customer compliance businesses can 'spy' on their customers using a number of techniques including the placement of cookies on customers' computers. It is in this manner that businesses which have several sites offering related and complementary products and services – thus engaging in link or affiliate marketing – know exactly where customers have been, when and for how long have they visited specific websites, what they have searched for, looked at and bought. This in turn provides customer compliance businesses with the necessary data to practise individual marketing and micromarketing as part of an interactive, continuing dialogue.

Some research undertaken by customer compliance businesses seems to be outsourced to their partners. 'Partners' here describes neither specialist research providers, such as research and market intelligence agencies, nor business partners that are closer along the industry value chains to end consumers and are thus in a better position to collect valuable information on consumers. With increasing quantities of data freely available online, businesses have learnt to make use of such data and, where possible, involve customers in the provision of valuable knowledge about themselves without the active involvement of the company. An example of such research outsourcing to customers is blogging. We will not discuss the matter of blogs in detail. However, it is noteworthy that blogs are increasingly described as 'knowledge repositories' into which companies can 'tap' in order to access the 'experiences, opinions, and needs' of their customers.[29]

Mehta and Sivadas (1995) were among the first to argue that the Internet may be useful when conducting empirical research, qualitative and ethnographic research in particular. Customer compliance businesses provide empirical evidence in support of such expectations. As already noted, they use the Internet as a prime observation tool. Internet community forums as an information gathering method have remained relatively untapped until recently.[30] Nonetheless, their growth mirrors the evolution in consumer-to-consumer relationships and attests to their current influence on brand choice. Consumer-to-consumer relationships which affect customer compliance business operations include online discussion forums, panels, chat rooms, lists, blogs, boards, virtual communities, online tribes and online brand communities. As recently demonstrated by Ryanair, which decided to use Facebook in an attempt to carry out research on its customers, consumer-to-consumer technological solutions can be harnessed by businesses to gather customers' views and understand customer experiences about service provision and service failure, at a fraction of the cost of personally contacting and even visiting dissatisfied customers. The effect of viral marketing is similar – it has proved successful and low cost, obviating the need for traditional research practices[31] by relying upon consumer interaction and engagement focused on social community websites such as Facebook and Friendster or by designing and building brand sponsored blogs.[32]

We have observed some customer compliance businesses setting up so-called company sponsored online forums and discussion panels known as blogs, prompting discussants to share their views on service provision, service information and preferences. When customers interact with other customers and discuss service provision, direct and relevant information can be obtained. Thus, there is less need to use specialised focus group settings, as done in traditional research. Similarly, social networks have grown as an avenue for conducting research, due to their increased popularity among customers. Customer compliance businesses such as Ryanair and IKEA seem to have recognised that interactions among customers in online communities enhance identification with specific brands.[33]

It has been suggested that secondary data may act on its own as a reliable foundation for research. Only anecdotal evidence exists of customer compliance businesses constructing databases by combining in-house records and secondary information available from external sources. Although during start-up customer compliance businesses may use secondary data by purchasing email address lists in order to assess the market that they attempt to target, established businesses seem to prefer to build and use their own proprietary databases. An example is the previously mentioned practice of using websites to ask visitors to provide details through the log-in facilities. Some websites do not even allow access without visitors revealing their identity and providing details that are added to company databases. Databases are also being built through the above mentioned link marketing and affiliate marketing. Affiliate marketing is an established method of obtaining business, but it works particularly well for online businesses because the link can be hidden from the consumer through designing a different Internet page which backs the same website. For instance, low-cost airlines generate sales from car hire, hotel booking, insurance, mobile phone services and even financial services and gambling (e.g., Ryanair bingo). Ryanair seems to have dropped its attempt to sell utilities, as this service no longer appears on their website – another interesting example of market research by what we call trial marketing (trial and error). It is also low-cost research, when compared to the expense of intelligence gathering through traditional methods such as test marketing.

In a 2006 article in *Travel Trade Gazette*, Caroline Baldwin, Ryanair's deputy head of Sales and Marketing at the time, noted that the company's in-house marketing team of 29 people did not carry out much market research but used 'common sense'. We are inclined to view this comment as further evidence of our thinking. Many customer compliance businesses seem to have research practices which may be described as bare market and marketing research, stripped to the basics, relentlessly cost-oriented, yet highly effective.

## Case in Point – Research, the 'easy' way

Back in 2007, easyJet's brand communications manager Andrew Berks commented: 'we are now in a much better position to track the performance of our marketing campaigns, in terms of understanding which Web content delivers the smartest conversion to bookings, from a low-fares flight to a holiday deal on our new easyJet holidays site'.[34] This had been achieved by easyJet using Webtrends, in an attempt to investigate and understand better customer behaviours and decisions and thus target them more effectively. Webtrends not only integrated the information collected from all of easyJet's websites but also brought together activities across websites and provided company staff with a more complete understanding of web analytics.

---

*Section summary for managers:*

o *Entrepreneurial customer compliance businesses use database marketing, Internet and call-centre technologies to continuously carry out market and marketing research.*
o *Research through listening to complaints is replaced with data mining and analysis of databases, real-time e-marketing research, trialling new products and identifying new market opportunities.*
o *Customer compliance businesses tend to automate and simplify data gathering and analysis.*

---

## 5.3 Research innovations and strategic thinking of customer compliance businesses

The innovations in research through automated marketing are at the heart of the innovativeness and success of customer compliance businesses. We have put together all of these innovations in a model (see Figure 5. 1) which illustrates innovative intelligence-gathering thinking. By taking full advantage of automated marketing and technological developments also available to their competitors, these companies appear to have inverted long-standing market and marketing research practices.

In order to make sense of these innovations and their implications for research and strategic decision-making, we draw attention to the Editorial in a recent edition of an important practitioner outlet in the UK – *Journal of Direct, Data and Digital Marketing Practice* (Vol. 9, No. 4, April–June 2008, 319–20). The Editorial discusses the need to bridge the gap between academic and practitioner research and knowledge. Although not being the only discussion dedicated to such an important matter, we draw attention to a problematic raised by the Editor. Knowledge, the reader is reminded, 'is best nurtured by gradual accumulated building ... or by daring to jettison received wisdom when it no longer meets changed circumstances' (p. 397–8). Having analysed the innovative practices of customer compliance businesses, our feeling is that

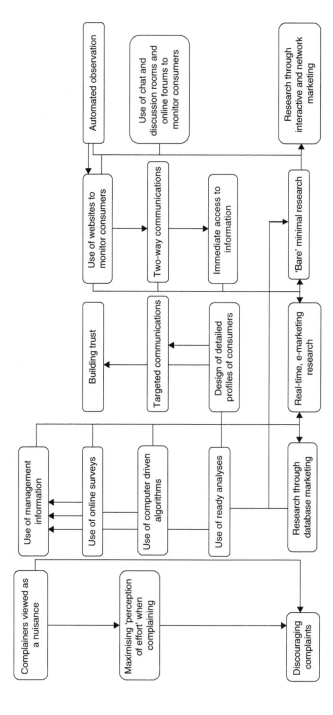

Figure 5.1  **The innovative automated marketing research practices of customer compliance businesses**

marketing has not recognised and documented adequately important innovations carried out by these companies in areas of data gathering, data analysis and application of data to decision-making. Yet these technology-driven research innovations have re-written much of what one finds about current best practice as regards research design, implementation, and evaluation.

Theorists and practitioners studying trends in carrying out and using research will need to analyse conceptually, empirically and in detail the ways in which customer compliance businesses have reversed thinking about carrying out research not by contacting dissatisfied customers and not by obtaining feedback from them. Such research practices can be explained only to an extent by a cost reduction mentality. More importantly, they are driven by a highly distinctive compliance business philosophy and have been enabled by recently introduced reliable, accurate tools of capturing trends, perceptions, and behaviours. Instead of relying upon personal contact and one-to-one methods of data collection, such businesses have embraced database marketing and have maximised the use of profiling past, existing and prospective customers. Applications of online automated marketing approaches to analyse customers and their needs and to build relationships with them should not be surprising, with website use dramatically increasing[35] and with ample data available to researchers through Internet marketing databases, search engines, and also newsgroups and blogs. All of these technology solutions and platforms empower managers – they can make decisions quickly while also saving time and reducing research costs, as done recently by Ryanair when it decided to use the online survey conducted by SKYTRAX (2008), and as observed by a minority of commentators.[36]

It should be clear by now that this has been a discussion not only of novel research practices but also of research which questions fundamentals of marketing philosophies underlying customer centricity. Far from endorsing customer centricity and conversations with unhappy and alienated customers, and contrary to normative calls for practitioners to encourage feedback by simplifying complaint procedures and minimising perceptions of effort on the part of complaining customers, customer compliance businesses have actively sought to discourage complaints and have resorted to research methods which remove complainers from processes of intelligence gathering.

---

### Chapter summary for managers:

o *Customer compliance carries out automated and innovative market and marketing research, not by listening to and researching complainers but by viewing them as a nuisance and ignoring them, opting instead for lower-cost methods of research and analysis.*

o *Automated research incorporates readily available management data and information, online cheaper methods of data collection and computer-driven algorithms or ready analyses.*

o *The twin features of discouraging complaints and extensive use of real time e-marketing research are central to the 'bare' market and marketing research undertaken by customer compliance businesses.*

# 6 Innovations in Business Model and Strategy

<br>

---

**Key questions in this chapter:**

o *How would you describe the business model of your company?*
o *Has your business recently revised or updated its business model in response to moves by your competitors?*
o *Do your business model and business level strategy take into account latest technology and communications developments and incorporate these?*
o *Can you identify promising new value streams and ways of simplifying your supply chain?*

---

## 6.1 The concepts of business model and e-business model

Marketing and strategy scholars have long conceptualised business models, generating separate and substantial literatures on this subject matter. The 'business model' concept is very much in vogue, with practitioner and conceptual analyses originating in theories of value chains, value systems and strategic positioning, resource-based theory,[1] the notion of Schumpeterian creative destruction, strategic network theory and transaction costs economics,[2] among others. This is a voluminous, diverse and growing field, in spite of its late arrival in academic thought[3] and the lack of consensus about the meaning of the concept. Definitions of what constitutes and describes business models most accurately vary, and the concept remains somewhat unclear.[4] A business model is also seen at times as a set of related components and strategies used to generate and grow resources and offer customers good value. Mitchell and Coles[5] view it as 'a way of organizing' which facilitates service provision.

There is also a lack of agreement about the ingredients of business models. Certain practitioners list customer orientation, strategic goals, processes, collaboration, technology and legal issues. Alternative views incorporate products and services, actors, roles, information, revenues and benefits. Dubosson-Torbay, Osterwalder and Pigneur[6] highlight sources of income, resources, collaborative networks, intimacy and brands which facilitate relations with customers – rather different from Mitchell and Coles'[7] preference for a conceptualisation of business models in terms of a series of questions: 'who', 'what', 'when', 'where', 'why', 'how' and 'how much', as viewed by stakeholders. Readers are reminded that great leaders do not 'simply build' but 'continually remodel' the ways in which their organisations add value for key stakeholders. Innovations in business models provide companies with longer-term advantage, unlike the shorter-term effects of technological innovation. Thus, although a fundamental, and foundational, understanding of business models is still to be uncovered and approved, an agreement has been reached that novelty in business models positively contributes to firm performance and value creation.[8] Irrespective of how practitioners and academics view and define business models, innovation is a consistent 'design theme' of business models, notwithstanding differences in theorising innovation as designed and carried out in terms of 'conducting transactions', 'connecting previously unconnected parties', 'linking transaction participants in new ways' or 'designing new transaction mechanisms'.

Recent advances in technology, communications and IT, of which customer compliance businesses have also taken advantage, have prompted the emergence of boundary-spanning forms of management and organising which have fundamentally reorganised economic exchange. New e-business models are founded upon a blend of value streams (value propositions of the company, including reduced product search costs and transaction costs), revenue streams (revenue generation) and logistical streams (supply chain designs).[9] E-business models are rather distinct from more general and traditional offline business models, with e-businesses relying on the Internet to buy, sell and serve customers. The short history of thinking about e-business models suggests that we may be far from the point in theorising time when the dust settles down and a commonly used term becomes common. At present, we read about Internet business models,[10] B2B business models,[11] electronic commerce business models and e-business models,[12] among others, adding to the considerable confusion in the area. Similarly, there is a surplus of classifications of e-business models. Some typologies help distinguish among models by using variables such as degree of innovation and functional integration, with some of the 'types' discussed being e-shops, e-procurement, e-auctions, e-malls and virtual communities. A very different approach seems to have been taken by writers such as Wirtz and Lihotzky[13] who prefer to theorise content-oriented, commerce-oriented, context-oriented and connection-oriented e-business models. Particularly important to our line of thinking, though, are suggestions that e-business models with 'dual core strategies' (e.g., 'comparative advantage' and 'concentration') tend to perform better than those relying upon a single 'core strategy'.[14]

There is also considerable disagreement about what makes some models successful – a question which, it seems, will preoccupy thinking in the practitioner and scholarly communities in the near future. Competitiveness of Internet business models has been variably attributed to innovative entrepreneurship and access to complementary assets through strategic partnerships and information sharing. For example, Zott, Amit and Donlevy[15] argue that e-business models create value through efficiency (supply chain re-design, provision of a vast set of products or services, time savings, transaction convenience and the reduction of information asymmetry) and 'stickiness' (by drawing and retaining customers through rewarding customer loyalty, personalising offers to customers, building virtual communities and developing online trust). Although contested in some circles, this framework was further developed in Amit and Zott's[16] study which identified four sources of value creation: efficiency, complementarities, lock-in and novelty.

---

### Section summary for managers:

o *There is a lack of consensus about the nature and elements of business models, though business models are often described in terms of strategic goals, processes, collaboration and resources, among others.*

o *Innovating one's business model provides the business with longer-term advantage over its competitors. Therefore, it is novelty more than any other feature of business models that positively affects value creation and performance.*

o *E-business models are described in terms of their value, revenue and logistical streams. The more successful e-business models seem to rely on dual core strategies.*

---

## 6.2   The customer compliance business model

Compared to existing as well as past business models, we view the business model of the customer compliance businesses as being primarily marked by innovations in four areas:

1. Process and partnering;
2. Use of merchant partners and link marketing;
3. Flat management structures, cultural openness and democratisation;
4. Transformational leadership.

It is in these four areas that the innovative thinking of customer compliance businesses appears to be most potent and contributing most to their success and competitiveness. Innovations across the above noted areas also 'fit' well together – there is consistency across them as innovative business model components, and they also match external conditions across sectors, with many of the business model innovations being driven by external and especially technological developments, as explained in preceding sections. As such, the four areas represent a 'holistic configuration' with a consistent 'theme' running across areas, which makes this customer compliance business model distinct and easily recognisable.

## 6.2.1   Processes and partnering

The first business model ingredient combines operational and strategic considerations, and covers innovations that customer compliance businesses have introduced in areas of process management and the use of extensive partnering arrangements. Our thinking is best illustrated with some more prominent examples, including low-cost airline customer compliance businesses using secondary and uncongested airports, controlling sales and administrative costs and employing multi-skilled staff. EasyJet's business model is driven by efficiency considerations, with both the founder and the current management team trying to identify costs which could be further reduced. Not offering meals during the flight reduces costs, as does the tendency of this and similar airlines to order a single type of aircraft and to fly from smaller, uncongested airports such as Luton, Charleroi, Bergamo, Prestwick and Weeze, helping achieve fast turnarounds. Business class seats are not being offered either, as part of a 'no freebies' mentality, thus increasing seating capacity and helping achieve frugality with respect to operations.

Swedish furniture retailer IKEA is another case of a customer compliance business which has invented new operations management practices in its industry – across areas of retailing, sourcing and logistics. This marks an attempt to combine lower-cost provision and high levels of customer service, in addition to various aspects of differentiation such as 'prosumption'. As a result, the company is recognised for its low prices and innovative design.

Yet another customer compliance business, Ryanair, has long competed successfully by forming a series of partnerships, over the years, with businesses operating across sectors. The company developed an extranet with its channel partners, in order to manage its wide distribution system more effectively.[17] In 2007, Ryanair signed an agreement with Gavitect AG, allowing this customer compliance business to provide a mobile ticket text service. Ryanair passengers could now book tickets, with ticketing barcodes sent to their mobile phones instead of them having to print out and produce paper-based tickets with barcodes clearly visible and machine readable. According to the terms of the agreement, Gavitect AG was expected to provide scanners to verify these bar codes. Ryanair passengers could also use the ticket text website to search for events across the continent. As argued by Santina Doherty, Ryanair's Head of Ancillary Revenue, this presented passengers with an exciting opportunity to do one-stop shopping of flights, hotels, cultural events such as concerts and live events.[18] In 2009, Ryanair was also the first carrier to offer mobile phone services on board in association with the on board mobile phone system provider OneAir. This service was trialled on the London-Dublin route, using satellite technology. Although this experiment ultimately failed, with the service discontinued in March 2010, the company has not given up its search for providers of identical and similar services.[19] Illustrative is the 2009 contract signed with Cable & Wireless,

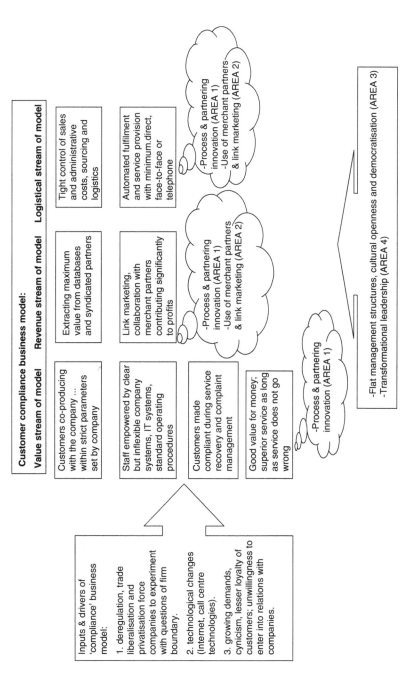

Figure 6.1  **Customer compliance business model innovations**

to manage the telecommunication network of the carrier in a deal worth some €15m.

Ryanair's collaborations with web analytics companies are not particularly well documented. One instance of such partnering is the agreement signed with AT Internet, to obtain feedback on, analyse and improve the use of the company's website by its customers. This collaboration and the lessons learnt by Ryanair's management allowed the business to redesign its website and its homepage in particular, to drive traffic more effectively to its ancillary partners, and foster conversion.[20] The partnering in question allegedly provided Ryanair with 'a 360° view' of the company, and assisted operational and strategic management not only on matters of web analytics but also online intelligence. Key performance indicators were identified and optimised, data were integrated, CRM was improved, and the company's email marketing activities were revisited. Heat maps were generated to determine the locations of greatest use by customers on Ryanair's website, allowing management to know what information and services customers looked up and clicked through. As a result, the number of click points was reduced and the click trajectory was improved when customers demonstrated eagerness to explore or use the ancillary services provided by the company's partners. A 16 per cent increase in ancillary revenues was reported. AT Internet also helped Ryanair assess the return on email campaigns launched by the company by cross-checking PNR (passenger name record) with financial data. Revenue generation was detailed in this manner, customer behaviours were optimally tracked, and information was extensively used for strategic decision-making purposes.

The link marketing activities of customer compliance businesses and their ability to offer ancillary services optimise offers and improve the direct dialogue with customers who are interested in one-stop shopping experiences. Link marketing hides complex relational networks that such companies weave in an attempt to offer ever more improved and better services to customers. Ryanair has a contractual agreement with Hertz, with Hertz paying the airline a per-passenger fee. Similar are the arrangements of the airline with Booking.com, for offering accommodation services. Financial service provision relies on contracts with MBNA and GE Capital Bank. The list can go on, and can be extended to other customer compliance businesses. The important point, though, is that such novel practices and offers would not be possible without re-defining processes, through partnering and relations as part of Area 1 innovations of the customer compliance business model. Commentators frequently remind us of the value of collaborations and partnerships as organisational resources and a source of attaining external valuable resources.[21] The strategic networks that customer compliance businesses develop with suppliers and other business partners illustrate this importance of materials, procurement, supply chain management and link marketing to their business models. By using their partners smartly, opportunities are generated for rich information flows,[22] the delivery of additional revenue at a minimal cost, and maximum value creation that harnesses in-house data.

Additional, and considerable, process investments have been carried out by many customer compliance businesses to automate sorting and stock management, and speed up purchase and delivery. Amazon, for instance, generates much revenue from syndicated partners such as Office Depot and Toys R Us. Its dominance may be partly explained by Amazon's success in convincing potential partners of the soundness of the company's business model. Consequently, companies such as Office Depot and Toys R Us are drawn into the Amazon way of thinking which espouses openness above secretiveness – illustrated by the access that Amazon's partners have to the proprietary software and electronic interfaces of the company. Amazon's proprietary procurement software and the company's heavy investment in systems of automated sorting and real-time market research rely on coordination with companies like Toys R Us. The software is shared, based on trust in the Amazon brand. With many of the companies selling through Amazon also being its direct competitors, Amazon's is a compelling case of building advantage by re-thinking traditional competition norms, by enhancing transparency of transactions, and by simplifying these very transactions.

It should be clear by now that the customer compliance business model relies on harnessing and combining the resources of one's business partners and customers. Such process re-organisation and partnering underlie IKEA's highly sophisticated sourcing strategy, focused not only on the control of costs of raw materials and components but also resting on the view that all suppliers and the company's customers are its key stakeholders. It may be useful to remember that at the time of IKEA's entry into the European furniture industry, the industry was fragmented and was marked by the prominence of second-hand sales and the passing-over of expensive furniture items across generations. IKEA's founder, Ingvar Kamprad, revolutionised the industry by replacing this model with one of affordable, relatively high quality, and modern yet simple furniture which would be immediately available to consumers to pick up and take home. The timely manufacture and delivery of such furniture items at prices which appeal to younger consumers meant that both production and supply would rest on developing and nurturing healthy, long-term relations with suppliers in Sweden and, more recently, in developed and especially developing countries.

We conclude this discussion with a few additional examples of process re-organisations and partnering. Exemplary is eBay's alliance with Yahoo in 2005 which was created so that the companies would collaborate in areas of web and sponsored search, by combining the strengths of the two competitors. Earlier in its history, eBay worked with AOL and GeoCities in order to achieve its 'Triple A's' – acquisition, activation and activity. A number of joint ventures were formed in the late 1990s and early 2000s with Compaq, NEC and Sun Microsystems. Apart from the aggressive acquisition programme that eBay has pursued ever since, its partnering and strategic alliance programme with other household brands has contributed much to the rapid growth of the company, allowing it to keep transaction fees under control, gain access to various sales channels, and enhance its reputation.

---

**Section summary for managers:**

o *The business model of customer compliance businesses relies heavily on partnering arrangements with companies, some of which are even direct competitors of these businesses.*

o *A key aspect of partnering is link marketing whereby customers' clicks through website links hide complex relational networks and shared commissions across compliance and non-compliance businesses, delivering additional revenue for these companies at minimal to no cost.*

o *Customer compliance businesses have developed new types, closer integrated relationships with suppliers and other businesses – syndicated partners sometimes with combined databases.*

o *Critical to the success of these businesses are the re-defined relations and processes of working with customers which combine control through compliance as well as substantial benefits to those customers who are willing and ready to comply with company expectations and procedures.*

---

### 6.2.2 Use of merchant partners and link marketing

Closely related to the issue of collaboration of customer compliance businesses with business partners is the above-noted extensive use of link marketing. The primacy, to customer compliance businesses, of link marketing and collaboration with merchant partners within symbiotic relationships, is not a new development in the business world. Link marketing, as practised by customer compliance businesses, rests upon traditional 'network externalities' – the more customers and other stakeholders use the activities of a provider, the greater the value of the service offers of that provider – long noted by commentators with respect to the advantages of collaboration. Being designed and implemented in association with key partners, link marketing is used so that customer compliance businesses get maximum coverage and contact with customers. Tesco's success is often attributed in part to cross-selling. In a similar fashion, and as pointed out elsewhere in the book, Ryanair and easyJet collaborate with car rental companies, hotels, life insurers, and mobile phone companies. All of these 'linked' activities earn companies commissions from selling additional services to customers. Particularly profitable are Ryanair's links with hospitality establishments (hotels and providers of various types of accommodation including self-catering and campsite holidays), travel service providers (car rental companies and cruise holidays companies, among others), financial and affiliated service providers (credit card providers and life insurers), communications service providers (mobile phone companies) and gift and gambling services (which have been withdrawn at the time of writing this book).

Link marketing and collaborations with merchant partners have turned the websites of many customer compliance businesses into one-stop shopping

Exhibit 6.1 **An example of link marketing and ancillary services offered by customer compliance businesses**

experiences, ideal for busy customers who constantly seek enhanced trans-action cost efficiencies by saving search effort and time but also by increas-ing the total value of an offer simply because bundles of offers end up being tailor-made and suited to specific momentary individual needs. Therefore, it should not be surprising that Ryanair's website alone gets over 600m page-views per month, making it one of Europe's largest booking websites. The mere fact that so many ancillary services are being offered on such web-sites also makes it easier for these companies to sell additional services. An interesting, recent example is a holiday lettings site used by Ryanair to offer 'guaranteed best price' of holiday accommodation. Such offers built on the earlier discussed provision of ancillary services on the part of Ryanair and the high profitability associated with the provision of such services. The published accounts suggest that about 22 per cent of the company's total operating revenue in 2011 came from such ancillary services (GBP 550m as estimated by the IdeaWorks, the US-based research group).[23]

---

### Section summary for managers:

o *Customer compliance businesses extensively use link marketing and mer-chant partnering to extract additional income from their database.*

o *Link marketing and the use of merchant partners is not new and has been prac-tised by marketeers even in the nineteenth century; however, link marketing is now part of an open business model that has redesigned supply chains.*

---

### 6.2.3   Flat management structures, cultural openness and democratisation

Commentators have long recognised that innovation thrives in flat, flexible and decentralised organisational structures.[24] Elements of such structures are uncovered across customer compliance businesses. IKEA's thinking emphasises equality, with the company having a limited number of lay-ers, open plan office layout and informal style of communication.[25] There are only four organisational strata in between the CEO and the checkout cashiers and warehouse clerks. IKEA's structure has been described variably, as 'democratised' or as 'a reverse hierarchy' where customers and not the top management are seen as driving the company's initiatives – a good illustra-tion of views that organisational structures should rely on, and encourage, cross-functional cooperation and autonomy.

Similar structural flatness characterises other customer compliance busi-nesses, even if achieved through different means. Some innovative strategies and techniques that easyJet's management has utilised to keep the costs of operation low and to maintain as flat a structure as possible include the minimal use of permanent employees, employment of multi-skilled staff and extensive outsourcing. EasyJet's founder, Stelios Haji-Ioannou, consciously designed and defended a democratic culture marked by transparency, with all documents being scanned and available on the company's website for employees to refer to and check. At least in the early years following the establishment of the company, Stelios nurtured an inclusive corporate environment, of which the Friday barbecues were a major part. The Culture Committee of the company consisted of staff elected and assigned a major role in developing novel company procedures.

We have already referred to Amazon's culture as open and flexible, but Devi and Aruna[26] also describe it as 'feel friendly'. Much due to this reputation, Amazon can easily attract talented and versatile people, establishing a sense of belonging and community among its staff. As in the cases of Ryanair, easyJet and Amazon, it was eBay's top management and Meg Whitman in particular who developed a work culture of fun[27] – an archetypal customer compliance business culture which is entrepreneurial and which takes pride in its innovative thinking underlying every aspect of its operation.

## Case in Point – IKEA's organisational culture

IKEA's is an entrepreneurial organisational culture largely free of the constraints of inherited norms and rules. The company prefers to describe itself in terms of the values of 'togetherness', 'cost consciousness', 'respect' and 'simplicity', signifying the emphasis on 'partnering with people' – be it employees or other stakeholders such as IKEA's business partners.[28] Such company values are attributed to the 'character' of the area in Sweden where the founder, Kamprad, was born. Here is what IKEA has to say, on its website, about this 'genetic imprint' when describing the continuity with the Småland-way of life: 'Småland, where the company's founder was born and raised, can be easily identified as the source of our shared values.[29] Simplicity, humility, thrift and responsibility are all evident in the lifestyle, attitudes and customs of the place where IKEA began.'[30] The company and its founder allegedly share this penchant for hard work, frugality, self-reliance and egalitarianism. Company employees still remember how the founder used to shake hands with them, though not in the spotlights of TV cameras as we so frequently witness when reading the business press or watching a TV programme about high-profile visits of company CEOs to business facilities. The informality and common sense approach to running IKEA are reflected in the layout and daily running of company offices. There appear to exist certain casualness and 'humility before the task'.[31] Personal titles are reported to be absent on business cards, and managers are encouraged not to display signs of prosperity or conspicuous consumption. As far as we are aware, IKEA has not given up on the tradition of organising an 'Anti-bureaucratic Week' during which managers go to the shop floor and carry out ordinary tasks typically entrusted on front-line and back office employees. Personal responsibility is highly valued, as is initiative taking, including the soliciting of the views of staff for improvements in operations and other business functions (the famous 'Express Yourself' programme comes to mind).[32] Employees, irrespective of their position, keep on being referred to as 'co-workers', and managers and lower level staff share common premises, addressing one another rather informally.[33]

The vigour and vitality of such cultures partly rests on faithfully implementing the values and vision of the founder-entrepreneur. IKEA is frequently equated with its founder's work ethic. Similarly, Ryanair's culture appears to have been profoundly shaped by, and centred on, O'Leary's challenges to the norms and conventions and his belief that the company is a 'champion' of the people. Kelleher of Southwest airlines is the archetypal creator of this type of culture. His staff treat him as a 'cult leader' rather than a 'captain of industry'.[34] The managers at the top of many customer compliance businesses appear to be very different from the salaried managers of big companies and tend to create cultures which may be difficult to replicate[35] due to their dependence upon collective processes within unique organisational settings created by such entrepreneurial figures. The cultures of successful customer compliance businesses are uninhibited by path-dependent thinking which one often finds among their incumbent rivals. This type of culture has been credited with higher level learning based on expertise, self-development and creativity. Indeed, it may prove difficult to compete against a culture such as IKEA's, marked by democratic design, responsibility and a thorough Code of conduct (the IWAY).

---

**Section summary for managers:**

o *Customer compliance businesses tend to have flat management structures, sometimes incorporating no more than three levels of operations and decision making.*
o *Cultures of these businesses seem to be rather democratic and are marked by transparency, with substantial company information available to customers and employees.*

---

## 6.2.4   Transformational leadership

The key input of entrepreneurs to customer compliance operations has already been outlined; however, the discussion has not properly covered 'transformational leadership' and its place in the overall design and implementation of the cultures of customer compliance businesses as exemplary of 'market-driving cultures'.[36] Transformational men and women are found at the helm of quite a few customer compliance businesses. IKEA's founder has been characterised as a 'role model' of the company's 'brand values', including its 'simpleness'.[37] He has been credited with challenging traditional practices in the sector. The company allegedly still remains 'inspired' by him, although it is no longer the modest organisation that he established so long ago. IKEA employees are often described as exhibiting 'a near religious adherence' to the practices institutionalised by him. This type of leadership appears to profoundly motivate organisational members towards realising a shared vision. Transformational leadership is also responsible for infusing the aspirations and values of the entrepreneur-founder by actively shaping the outline of a culture appropriate for such growth-focused organisations. Transformational leadership appears to be particularly appropriate for businesses which are uninhibited by past resource and planning directions.

While incumbents across the sectors where customer compliance businesses have appeared and prospered aspire to emulate such transformational leadership, they are frequently led by senior 'professional managers' who focus on short-term and moderate growth targets.[38] Successfully emulating the cultures of customer compliance businesses has proved a tricky task for traditional businesses even though, having set the parameters of such cultures, it becomes obvious that there is nothing conceptually and qualitatively new and unexplored or unexplained that such companies do so well. Rather, these 'cultures of excellence' are not so much marked by cleverness but by their ability to help create and maintain organisational processes, functions and routines which exceed the efficiency and effectiveness of those of their rivals.[39] The innovative organisations that we analyse successfully erect cultures of constant innovation, 'energy' and 'commitment' enabled and driven by charismatic leaders who often also happen to be founders, with a clear and novel agenda. The intensity of the vision is contagious, drawing and attracting others rather than forcing them to accept it.

The founder-entrepreneurs represent valuable and inimitable resources and capabilities. They are not only strategic leaders but also, at times, colourful or controversial personalities. Think of O'Leary. His signature comments have been extensively reported, commented upon, and analysed. He has been described as a manager who 'loves to float outrageous trial balloons'.[40] Some examples of such behaviour, which may be seen as rather outlandish, can be seen on several Youtube videos, where Ryanair's CEO is heard to suggest, during press conferences, 'to close immediately the aviation regulator's office', referring to them as 'useless idiots'.[41] During another press conference, while announcing the new Trans-Atlantic service to be offered by Ryanair, O'Leary describes the new offer as 'beds and blowjobs'.[42] The innovativeness in thinking of such founder-entrepreneurs and their ability to recognise, nurture and harness unique company resources are hard to replicate.

---

**Section summary for managers:**

o *Customer compliance businesses are often entrepreneurial companies which are recent arrivals to the sectors where they operate. In many cases, their founders are still running the business or are involved in a supervisory role.*

o *The managers who founded and run these businesses seem to be transformational leaders with management styles in sharp contrast to the styles of the salaried career managers running traditional businesses that are the direct competitors of customer compliance companies.*

o *Managers of customer compliance businesses are driven by the intensity of their vision which is contagious and attracts others.*

o *They are often outspoken, colourful and controversial personalities who seek publicity, especially if it benefits their companies.*

---

## 6.3   Strength and competitiveness of the customer compliance business model

The starting point of the book was the unprecedented success and growth of customer compliance businesses across sectors. Many have become household names and are strong, valued brands. In the mid 1990s, eBay reported staggering growth rates, sometimes reaching 70 per cent monthly growth. With such figures in hand, it was not surprising when the company announced over 150 million registered users by the second quarter of 2005. EBay's gross merchandise volume increased by 17 per cent in 2006, to USD 12.6 bn. Over 250 million people had traded using eBay from 1995 to 2003.[43] During the second quarter of 2006 alone, eBay boasted adding 10m new customers to its databases.[44] Similarly, from its IPO in 1997, Amazon has defied analysts' expectations that it would not be able to compete successfully against Barnes & Noble and other retailers. Only two years after the IPO, its market value had exceeded the combined value of Barnes & Noble and Borders. In 1995 Amazon had only 11 employees; by 1999 the figure was 2,100, while in 2012 they had more than 56,000 employees.[45] Another customer compliance business analysed here, IKEA, has become the world's largest designer and retailer of furniture. Today, the company operates more than 160 stores. It has been consistently ranked by *Business Week* and *BrandChannel* among the strongest global brands and those brands enjoying the highest levels of customer awareness. Commentators claim that the company 'has succeeded over the last twenty five years to do what no furniture distributor has ever attempted: to become a global player in an industry considered by nature to be local'.[46] Last but not least, easyJet operated a fleet of six Boeing 727-300's in early 1998. By the following year, the fleet had trebled and the number of routes – more than doubled. The sustained success that followed was evidenced by consistent growth indicators. In 2002, the company signed a contract with Airbus to deliver 120 aircraft to the company. Another milestone in this relentless trajectory of growth was the announcement in July 2002 that the company had served for the first time 1 million passengers in a single month.[47] By 2007, the company was a proud owner of 137 aircraft in total. Just like its customer compliance rival Ryanair, easyJet boasts strong sales and profitability.

Sustainable competitive advantage can originate in operational effectiveness (doing what one's competitors do, but better) or strategic positioning (delivering unique value to customers by doing things differently from one's competitors). As regards strategic positioning – the area where customer compliance businesses have innovated most, and contrary to common perceptions in the literature of the centrality of operational effectiveness – commentators suggest that the companies that we refer to as customer compliance businesses operate on the basis of cost leadership alone.[48] Such analysts seem to misunderstand the service focus and differentiation of customer compliance businesses as a current, highly successful example of 'hybrid'[49] and 'market driving'[50] companies. They flourish by combining cost leadership, differentiation (a combination of superior customer responsiveness, innovation, and quality) and focus (targeting carefully their messages to specific individuals through automated software systems). They have forcefully emerged into prominence and dominance in their sectors, either in their role of 'high growth start-ups' or 'revolutionaries'.

It is also clear that customer compliance businesses share some of the traits of disruptive e-business models, with their key distinguishing feature being service provision. As with other e-business models,[51] the customer compliance business model relies both on 'critical incidents', as much as offline businesses do,[52] and customer involvement in co-production. However, as already discussed elsewhere in this book, these companies have inverted the norms governing 'critical incidents' in areas of complaint management and service recovery. This is the unifying 'design theme'[53] of their business model identified by us. It is also the 'design theme' emphasised most throughout the book. Referring to Figure 6.1, the innovations that are part of the customer compliance business model are a 'blend' of value streams, revenue streams and logistical streams, illustrating the possibility of competitive advantage by adopting e-business models with dual core strategies which combine cost leadership and differentiation, and which continue to be successful even during the current economic downturn, at a time when many other companies have either not grown or have contracted.

---

### Chapter summary for managers:

o *Customer compliance businesses have grown dramatically in the past decade.*

o *Thanks to innovative business models, these companies appear to have achieved competitive advantage over traditional businesses across a number of sectors.*

o *The business level strategies of customer compliance businesses are hybrid – a combination of cost leadership and differentiation, with focus, and not solely cost leadership as suggested by some commentators.*

o *Although not defined as customer centric, in the traditional sense of this term, customer compliance businesses effectively meet customer needs through innovation, quality and value for money service.*

# 7 Reactions to Customer Compliance Businesses

---

**Key questions in this chapter:**

o *Do you really know what your customers think about your company, including its ethics and social responsibility?*
o *Have you measured the effect of customer ratings, blogs and online criticism on your businesses?*
o *Do you think that corporate reputation and negative media coverage can undermine your brand?*
o *Do you feel that pleasing complaining customers represents value for money for your company and that addressing all their concerns will positively affect the financial position of your business?*

---

## 7.1 Corporate reputation, media coverage and word of mouth

Social accountability and ethics seem to be two concepts which figure prominently on the radar of most companies these days. Practitioners are often warned that failure on the part of businesses to recognise the significance of accountability and meet ethical requirements would generate adverse media coverage and customer backlash. This gradual though dramatic change in expectations towards private-sector businesses has been at times attributed to consumers' sensitisation to controversial issues, ethical standards of corporate behaviour and growing reports of private sector abuses. One does not need to carry out extensive search on news items or analyses articles to come across stories about 'irresponsible managers' and 'greedy bankers' – a rather fashionable topic, following the credit crunch which started in the USA in 2008 and spread to the rest of the world. Just as 'ethics', 'social responsibility' and 'stakeholder management', notions of 'word of mouth' (and 'word of mouse' (WoM)) have been extensively reported and assessed across contexts, through consumer behaviour, services marketing, relationship marketing, marketing communication and strategy lenses.

One of the most fruitful traditions in accountability, corporate ethics, managerial morality and organisational reputation has also supplied some of the fundamental questions and challenges about service provision that this book attempts to tackle – service failure, service recovery and complaint management. It has already been noted that scholars working in this area have long claimed that, following the experience of a service defect, the provider should attempt to mitigate the negative effect of the failure by compensating, empathising or apologising to the affected customer.[1] If the customer feels disappointed with the response of the company, its procedures of dealing with complaints, or the approach and attitude of front-line staff in charge of making amends, the customer's negative evaluation may be reaffirmed, possibly resulting in an exit and his or her sharing the experience with friends, colleagues, and family member.

An acceptable and desirable scenario, to most academics working in areas of services and relationship marketing, is for the customer to feel a distinct sense of satisfaction with the response and the post-failure actions of the provider. According to this scenario, the customer may hopefully form positive post-recovery evaluations of the provider, the service and the service recovery process and outcome. Loyal customers are supposedly less motivated to search for alternative products and services and are less likely to feel attracted by the communication messages and persuasion attempts of rival brands,[2] even if they have experienced service defects and unsatisfactory incidents of 'difficult' interaction with company staff at some point in the past. To Wirtz and Mattila,[3] satisfied and loyal customers act as 'facilitators'. They generate positive word of mouth, and tend to share their experiences with companies, products, service offers and brands to which they feel attached. Therefore, we can confidently conclude that a significant majority of researchers in services marketing view secondary satisfaction as a powerful stimulus for future purchase intentions and re-patronage on the part of customers as well as their readiness to share such 'good news' with members of their close social circles. To some academics, this is precisely the type of customer loyalty which affects longer-term competitive advantage of companies.[4]

Analyses of corporate accountability, ethics, reputation, word of mouth and their effect on re-patronage, competitive advantage and company profitability have proliferated in digital marketing and e-marketing as well. Electronic word of mouth is defined in very similar terms, as 'any positive or negative statement made by potential, actual, or former customers about a product or company, which is made available to a multitude of people and institutions via the Internet'.[5] The impact of this so-called e-WoM is explained by the propensity of consumers to socially connect, interact with, and primarily get influenced by other consumers who are members of online communities and tribes of like-minded people. Mostly for the same reasons as in the offline environment, when we act as members of such communities, we also seek advice and use other members as sources of information.[6] In an environment where the consumer cannot touch and experience the product or service and where financial, social and physical risks multiply, information from a trusted source appears to be highly prized and sought. As Hennig-Thurau et al.[7] rightly point out, online opportunities for seeking and obtaining advice are potentially limitless. Consequently, as in the offline environment,[8] the effectiveness of WoM (or rather, e-WoM) is at least partly a product of one's strength of social ties. It is unnecessary to suggest that strong relationships are considerably more influential in terms of the effect they have and, consequently, the e-WoM they generate. The specific techniques and tools used to transmit recommendations and views – such as blogs, web-based discussion forums, social networking sites, chat rooms, websites, communities, newsgroups or emails – are not that critical. More significant is the alleged role that they play in maintaining or destroying company fortunes.

Similarly, more recent contributions to the marketing communications literature have increasingly placed the emphasis, in terms of the influence and effectiveness of informing or persuading audiences, on the use of more informal channels to communicate messages. Recognition of the significance of WoM is certainly not a new feature of this or any other stream of marketing research. Communication theorists and practitioners have long identified the effectiveness of WoM-based communications due to customers' perceptions of WoM credibility and reliability. Word of mouth is allegedly free from corporate interests, intervention and manipulation.[9] In the case of reference groups, though, the effectiveness of the advice received through WoM is predicated on the perceived trustworthiness of the source but also to the (perceived) expertise of the source. It is more likely that the consumer would approach the information provided by important others with greater confidence, based on one's conviction that the information sender is providing not only unbiased but also accurate, complete and up-to-date information.

---

### Section summary for managers:

o *Practitioners are frequently warned, by academics and social commentators, that failure to observe expectations of accountability and meeting the ethical expectations of their customers and the general public would generate negative media coverage and negative customer perceptions.*

o *Expectations about corporate ethics, morality and responsible behaviour dictate that service failures should be addressed in a timely and satisfactory manner, pleasing affected customers.*

---

## 7.2 The negative reaction to customer compliance businesses in the media

Most of the companies that are being discussed here have been involved in controversy at some point in their recent history and have been subjected to unwelcome scrutiny and attention on the part of the general or business press. Some of IKEA's suppliers in less-developed countries such as India have been found to use child labour. The company also acknowledged that some of its timber and furniture suppliers had been implicated in illegal logging, thus questioning the green credentials of the company and its code of conduct. It should be pointed out that the 2007 admittance of improper practices within IKEA's business network followed revelations about such practices published by the BBC and commentators, following lengthy investigations of illegal logging practices and deforestation preceded by similar reports in the late 1990s and early 2000s.[10] The company had taken pride in its policies of ecological and community responsibility, best captured in the slogan that the low price of the products and services offered in the IKEA retail outlets had not been produced or delivered 'at any price'. IKEA's own investigation, which followed the incident and the widespread negative media publicity, revealed some falsification of documentation on the part of the company's suppliers in China. This was an important outcome of the company's own investigation, as IKEA had previously relied on its partners to submit inspection reports about internal practices. Subsequent revelations followed with respect to poor working practices and conditions in some of the company's Indian textiles and rugs suppliers. In its defence, the retailer noted that much of the production of such items took place in family homes, making control and inspection rather difficult to implement.[11]

IKEA had been plagued by equally grave and potentially destructive PR disasters a decade earlier. At the time, it seemed that the company had managed to rebuild a strong stakeholder responsibility agenda. In 1998, following allegations about poor working conditions prevalent on premises of Indian suppliers, IKEA had seemingly settled the matter by signing an agreement. A group had been formed to monitor work conditions. Three years later, the company had introduced its famous Code of Conduct,[12] clearly stipulating standards of acceptable work conditions and rules about employment as well as the use of child labour. IKEA had made available assistance to women working in its Indian supply outlets. In order to repair its image, the company had also started an initiative of founding 'bridge schools' for those children employed by the company's suppliers, and had been actively involved in providing micro credit to women.[13]

Past and more recent allegations have repeatedly forced the company to defend its record, with a number of press releases and considerable information on the company's philosophy and practices posted on its website. This is what IKEA has to say in its defence, on its website:

> Child labor does exist in countries where IKEA products are manufactured, but IKEA does not accept child labor at its suppliers or their sub-contractors. IKEA works actively to prevent child labor. We base our work on the United Nations Convention on the Rights of the Child (1989), which defines the basic principle of always putting the best interests of the child first. The work IKEA does in this regard is also based on the International Labor Organisation (ILO) Convention

number 138 (1973) concerning minimum working ages, and the ILO Convention number 182 (1999) concerning the worst forms of child labor.[14]

In order to defend its credentials as a business committed to social responsibility, the company has been recently publicising 'The IKEA Way on Preventing Child Labor'. Past practices of suppliers submitting documentation on internal management had been replaced with an independent monitoring undertaken by KPMG to ensure compliance with and adherence to this 'IKEA Way'. In order to communicate its philosophy more effectively to suppliers and other business partners, but also to understand better the concerns and realities of production and management that its suppliers in less developed countries faced, IKEA had also initiated a series of workshops involving suppliers. In case of non-compliance being detected by the company, IKEA was to enforce its 'corrective action plan' by working with the business partner to amend reported transgressions. Termination of a relationship, even with a long-term supplier, was now made possible if corrective action was not taken on the part of a supplier or if IKEA felt that any changes introduced were of inadequate level or quality.[15]

The opening of new IKEA stores is frequently followed by newspaper stories of long queues, stampedes, injuries and even deaths. Such incidents were documented by the process following the opening of some of the company's stores in the USA, after IKEA had organised in-store sleep sessions. The opening of the Edmonton store in North London in early 2005 attracted a crowd of 6,000 eager shoppers waiting for the promised substantial opening discounts which were to last for the first three working hours on that day.[16] Not surprisingly, the store opening resembled a river torrent in early spring, when watched on TV later that night. Enthusiastic Londoners elbowed their way into the store and engaged in queue-jumping to beat near competitors. Customers who had been queuing for hours for prized products could be seen charging the doors of the outlet, injuring other shoppers in the process of doing so.[17] This specific opening was not marred by fatalities – unlike the store opening in Saudi Arabia the previous year when three customers were literally crushed to death.[18] 'Crush chaos at Ikea store opening,' the BBC announced on 10 February 2005, in its commentary on the opening of the Edmonton store. When interviewed, as reported by the BBC, the Tottenham MP, David Lammy, attacked the company's approach to store openings by arguing that 'IKEA must have known that in opening the store next to the second most deprived constituency in London and by leafleting the area about knock down bargains for those who arrived first, people would flock to their store in large numbers'.[19] The CNN headline read 'Stampede Mars IKEA London Opening',[20] while *The Sun* exclaimed 'Riot at New IKEA Store', adding below the headline that 'Cops battled to stop a RIOT last night at the opening of an IKEA furniture store'.[21]

More recently, bribery allegations involving senior company managers have also contributed to the growing volume of bad press involving IKEA.[22] In 2010, the *New York Times* published an article on the dismissal of two senior company executives in Russia, following revelations that they had been implicated in 'allowing' a contractor to pay a bribe.[23] The executives were Per Kaufmann, IKEA's director for Eastern Europe, and Stefan Gross, the company's director shopping mall business in Russia. Although corruption of this type is common business practice in Russia, the newspaper reminded its readers, these revelations were damaging to a company which had long been at the vanguard of campaigning against governmental corruption. Interestingly, Per Kaufmann had previously issued a statement reiterating IKEA's firm stance on corruption in Russia and announcing the possibility of the company suspending future investments in that country. Following the *New York Times*'s revelations, IKEA's CEO expressed his 'deep upset' and 'disappointment' in a company statement, and the company promised to open an investigation of its operations in Russia.

The stories described so far should not surprise the readers. Any business of the size and influence of IKEA is likely to be subject to systematic scrutiny on the part of industry analysts, general commentators, investigative journalists and customers. However, the number of human resource management-related criticisms, the stories of operational weaknesses, and the magnitude of customer dissatisfaction as evidenced in negative viral marketing are compelling. From the company's perspective, the proliferation and growing aggression of blogs should be disconcerting – if marketing theory about corporate accountability, ethics and reputation is correct in its predictions. During a rather casual, 30 minute search of the Internet alone, the authors of this book came across and recorded in excess of 40 blogs, including 'IkeaAttack', 'I hate Ikea' on Facebook, 'Retail torture – Swedish style, 'Why I hate Ikea', 'I hate Ikea' on mySpace, and numerous videos uploaded on Youtube to this effect. Furthermore, some of these blogs seemed to attract considerable consumer attention and involvement, with certain blog entries boasting close to or exceeding 3,000 opinions. Many marketing academics would conclude that such websites and postings, when combined with the speed of online communication and the spread of news these days, could severely and even irreparably damage the image and reputation of a multinational.[24]

Moving away from the above examples involving IKEA, the presentation of customer compliance businesses more generally in national media may be seen as a cause for concern. The soundness of easyJet's decision to take place in the earlier mentioned *Airline* TV series had been questioned, especially at the start of the series, by many industry analysts and academics. Although the series has turned into a piece of highly successful marketing communications for the company, more challenging incidents involved negative publicity about overbooked flights, flight cancellations and resulting customer inconvenience and re-booking at short notice. The extent and frequency of negative coverage of easyJet, though, pales into insignificance when compared to the number of stories about Ryanair.[25] Examples include newspaper pieces and analyses in the press and in academic outlets following publicity stunts involving Michael O'Leary such as his 2003 heading an 'army' of staff and a World War II tank to Luton airport with the intention to 'liberate' easyJet's customers from the allegedly high prices paid by them. The company's controversial advertisements have been the subject of careful scrutiny and attention, not only on the part of the company's competitors. Ryanair has been described as a company that is 'no stranger to controversy',[26] and these concern not only service-related aspects of its operation[27] but also adverts.[28] No aspect of Ryanair's operation has been left not scrutinised and criticised over the past decade or so.

Telling is BBC's *Panorama* programme on Ryanair, aired on 12 October 2009. Jeremy Vine, *Panorama*'s presenter, introduced the company as the 'airline we love to hate'. The programme's team made a number of allegations about the company, including doing business on its own terms, cutting services that customers demanded, facing consistent problems with its corporate website (including its 'poor design'), the liability of a rude and objectionable CEO and the fact that customers had to use their own resources to obtain the service. One interviewee, Gary Davies, Professor of Corporate Reputation at Manchester Business School, argued that customers felt cheated if they were made to pay for a bag that was not checked online. You as a customer are fined if you do not do what Ryanair wants you to do, Davies noted, adding towards the end of the interview that the company should 'watch out' for signs of reduced trust in its business proposition. This BBC coverage is similar to the negative comments on and analyses about Ryanair's payment policy,[29] its 'free flights',[30] and the allegedly lowly place of the company in ethics rankings[31] as well as of other customer compliance businesses such as IKEA on the blogosphere where one finds numerous websites dedicated to such 'consumer activism', including dedicated Facebook groups. The questions that we will attempt to answer later in this chapter are whether negative publicity really affects the performance of customer compliance businesses and, consequently, whether publicity matters at the end of the day. First, though, we look at the negative reaction to customer compliance businesses in academic writings.

---

### Section summary for managers:

o Customer compliance businesses have been criticised by media, social commentators and academics for ignoring complainers and behaving unethically.

o Commentators and many academics seem to misunderstand the fundamentals of customer compliance, with difficult and costly complainers ignored and customers defined as 'good' being rewarded for not causing complications and thus adding to the cost of running these businesses.

o In spite of negative media coverage and criticisms, customers continue to buy the products and services offered by customer compliance businesses.

o Far from hiding the principles of their operation, many customer compliance businesses actually publicise their compliance procedures and seek to explain the logic of consequences of these procedures, including benefits to their customers.

o Therefore, 'educating' customers and the general public about principles of compliance is a prime objective of the communication strategies of these businesses.

## 7.3 Negative reaction in academia to, and misunderstanding of, customer compliance principles

Similar to the negative media coverage of customer compliance businesses is the significant misunderstanding of the principles of operation, and outcomes, of customer compliance in certain sections of marketing academia. Customer compliance businesses operating in air transportation in particular have been the target of considerable criticism, masking a lack of appreciation of the innovativeness of management and marketing thinking which continues to influence the design and implementation of the tools discussed in earlier chapters. Exemplary of such what we view as erroneous treatment and analysis is a recent blog on *Harvard Business Review*'s website, where Taylor (2009) quotes an earlier article on Ryanair in *The Economist*, accusing the company of a lack of consideration for its customers. To Taylor and many other academics, businesses practising what we refer to as customer compliance ignore customer needs and do not follow up complaints and customers' requirements. Here is what one finds, following a description of some of strengths of the company and its brand: 'Ryanair has become a byword for appalling customer service, misleading advertising claims and jeering rudeness towards anyone or anything that gets in the way'. Following Creaton's[32] line of argument, it is safe to say that this particular company's proposition is frequently confused and that it remains misconstrued. The airline tends to be described as cheap and nasty, with the focus typically being on the second of the two adjectives. Rather simplistic, for instance, is Binggeli and Pompeo's[33] assessment of Ryanair's approach as low cost and their view that the Ryanair customer is a bargainer and a low yield individual who would not have flown otherwise. Misconstrued analyses, evaluations and subsequent recommendations to customer compliance businesses are unlikely to influence the thinking of the management of these companies. Attempts on the part of academics to force customer compliance businesses to behave like traditional companies are thus likely to meet a similar fate as suggestions to Ryanair's O'Leary to 're-brand' his company. O'Leary's reaction to such recommendations was simple and resolute: 'We have no intention of changing the brand or redesigning the image or the rest of that old nonsense. In my thirteen years at this company, Aer Lingus has changed its branding three times, British Airways has changed it three times, we've changed it not once, and the virtue of what we've done has been proven.'[34]

Rather than suggesting a re-orientation in the thinking of managers of customer compliance businesses, we draw attention to Stalk and Lachenauer's[35] concept of 'hardball management' and Boru's[36] assessment of the success of companies such as Wal-Mart, Dell, Microsoft, Toyota and Ryanair, 'predicated on the take-no-prisoners ethos' and 'five forget-me-not fundamentals: focus relentlessly on competitive advantage (i.e. aim for constant improvement), strive for extreme competitive advantage (widen the performance gap), avoid attacking directly (sneaky does it), exploit people's will to win (maintain a war footing) and know the caution zone (keep it legal)' (p. 45). Stalk and Lachenauer's 'hardball management' approach which is not about 'cruelty' – for 'hardball' is 'tough' but it is 'not sadistic' – goes a long way in presenting aspects of thinking of top management in what we label customer compliance businesses, for the stance of companies like Ryanair reveals a company philosophy of the business world as a terrain where only the most disruptive strategic innovators[37] survive.

---

### Section summary for managers:

o *Some academics appear to be confused about the customer compliance business proposition.*

o *Certain academics seem to attempt to 'force' customer compliance businesses to behave in the way traditional businesses do, ignoring the fact that customer satisfaction underpins the rapid growth and profitability of customer compliance businesses.*

o *Customer compliance businesses focus relentlessly on achieving and sustaining their competitive advantage, seeking and implementing novel ways of delivering value and often meeting customer needs better than their competitors.*

---

## 7.4   The customers' views and reactions

In spite of negative attitudes and critical analyses in the general press and in academia, customer compliance companies have consistently fought back, publicising statistics demonstrating the high level of customer service provided by them. Considering that Ryanair views itself as a company that operates in the transport business – with the aim of transporting customers between points A and B on short-haul routes – it fares better than its legacy rivals on all important, tangible aspects of service provision, as exhibited in Table 7.1. The statistics suggest superior punctuality, fewer pieces of lost baggage and higher rates of completions than the select few incumbents in the industry shown on the table. Ryanair, it seems, is more reliable, in terms of the consistency of the core service provided by it. Even if the figures presented below are challenged since they have been generated internally by the company, the differences between Ryanair and traditional incumbents operating in the sector are exposed in independent rankings, such as that produced by Barrett.[38] Thus, one may argue that stories of weaker service provision downplay evidence of service improvements on the part of customer compliance businesses, including the relentless use of technology to invent creative ways of providing new services or services in novel ways so that to fulfil both existing and unmet customer needs and desires.

Ryanair's management have been particularly upfront about their view of unwelcome publicity and negative comments on various aspects of their operations. Rather than relying upon rumour, objective facts should be used to evaluate the services of customer compliance businesses. Ryanair,

**Table 7.1**   Service quality indicators of Ryanair against legacy airlines

| Airline | Bags mishandled or missing (per 1000), 2006* | % completions, 2009** | Average Delay (mins.), Jan-Dec 2008*** | Average Delay (mins.), Jan-Dec 2011*** | Over 1 hour late (%), Jan-Dec 2011**** |
|---|---|---|---|---|---|
| Ryanair | 0.3 | 99.0 | 12.3 | 8.1 | 1.7 |
| Lufthansa | 12.7 | 98.4 | 12.3 | 12.9 | 3.6 |
| British Airways | 18.9 | 97.9 | 17.6 | 10.8 | 3.2 |
| Air France | 16.9 | 96.9 | 15.4 | 9.0 | 2.2 |
| Alitalia | 19.6 | 99.2 | 16.1 | 9.9 | 2.5 |

Adapted from: (1). Eventplanning (http://eventplanning.about.com/od/transportation/a/airline-baggage-checked-baggage-lost-luggage_3.htm) and extract from AEA Consumer Report Dec 2006*; (2). Half-year results analyst briefing, Ryanair (2009)**; (3). Flightontimeinfo statistics 2008, 2011***; (4). Flightontimeinfo statistics 2011****.

for instance, was nominated the most popular airline on the Internet in 2004. The company has rather successfully managed customers' attitudes by altering attribute priorities. While air transportation used to be a glamorous activity accessible only to the rich, to Ryanair it is an instance of what we term 'democratised' service provision which, in Ryanair's case, assumes the format of point-to-point transportation available to most of us. New attributes of flying have also been added – ones which were not offered by its competitors, including technology-based services such as online check-in and Ryanair Direct, where tickets are sold through their telemarketing service. Such attitude-altering schemes have been highly successful, evidenced by the fact that customers seem to increasingly understand the fundamentals of their relationship with customer compliance businesses and are becoming increasingly accepting of such practices.

Comments found on multiple blog sites testify to how successful customer compliance businesses are in 'educating' their customers about the principles and benefits of their business principles. Customers have come to adopt even the language of compliance used by these companies, internalising the very discourse and rhetoric of redefined provider-customer relations. While commenting on the high-quality service provided by the specific customer compliance business, a customer and a former employee of a traditional rival of a customer compliance business noted: 'You just have to follow the rules. M.O.L. (*Michael O'Leary*) tells you how to "play" the rules.'[39] Accusations levelled at the company both in the press and by some academic commentators – of hidden charges and the unethical and dishonest management of customer interactions – have been re-assessed by bloggers. Here is what some of them have to say about aspects of customer compliance: 'we all

**Table 7.2** Customers' perceptions about incidences of customer compliance

| Issue studied | Operationalisation of issue | Airlines | Comms and telecoms | Finance & banking | Electronic retail | Travel |
|---|---|---|---|---|---|---|
| A. Extent of use of compliance (measure 1) | Number (and %) of respondents reporting service control of compliance type | 468 (37.6%) | 452 (36.3%) | 739 (59.4%) | 670 (53.9%) | 389 (31.3%) |
| B. Extent of use of compliance (measure 2) | % of respondents reporting service control of the compliance who have been with the service provider for more than 5 years | 29.5% | 28% | 55.5% | 32.5% | 15% |
| C. Extent of customers' acceptance of compliance (measure 1) | % of reporting respondents who have not complained | 63% | 35.5% | 45% | 39% | 44.5% |
| D. Extent of customers' acceptance of compliance (measure 2) | % of reporting respondents who have not complained but who will (or may) use the company's services in the future | 75.5% | 75% | 79% | 79% | 66.5% |
| E. Extent of customers' acceptance of compliance (measure 3) | % of reporting respondents, who have complained but who will (or may) use the company's services in the future | 51.5% | 55% | 72.5% | 77% | 43.5% |
| F. Compliance techniques (measure 1) | % of reporting respondents unable to find the company's complaint procedures (as % of respondents) | 55.8% | 56.5% | 59.7% | 60.1% | 79.4% |

| | | | | | |
|---|---|---|---|---|---|
| G. Compliance techniques (measure 2) | % of reporting respondents who have experience with past complaint to the company, with the company not doing anything, so customers find complaints are not worthwhile (as % of respondents) | 48.1% | 49.7% | 44.7% | 41.6% | 76.3% |
| H. Compliance techniques (measure 3) | % of cases when company invokes rules and complaining customer receives no compensation (as % of respondents) | 39% | 42% | 44% | 25.5% | 36% |
| I. Compliance techniques (measure 4) | % of cases when company does not apologise (as % of respondents) | 37% | 40% | 34.5% | 23.5% | 55.5% |
| J. Compliance techniques (measure 5) | % of cases when staff are being courteous and apologetic but stick rigidly to company procedures (as % of respondents) | 67.3% | 70.5% | 72.5% | 70.3% | 54.7% |
| K. Compliance techniques (measure 6) | % of cases when staff appear unconcerned and uncooperative and stick rigidly to company procedures (as % of respondents) | 60.9% | 64% | 54.3% | 53.2% | 57.1% |
| L. Compliance techniques (measure 7) | % of cases when the approach of staff does not vary in style and content depending on the person, call centre or department contacted (as % of respondents) | 79.9% | 55.3% | 66.7% | 83.7% | 74.1% |

Source: The authors' own research with a sample representative of the UK population (2010)

know that FR [Ryanair] have no hidden charges. How can they be hidden if you have to click a button that agrees to the amount? If you don't like the amount, then back track to reduce it or not pay it'.[40]

The media and some academics also share a misperception that customers are unable to evaluate the negative comments about customer compliance businesses in popular media outlets and in the academic press. In response to the earlier mentioned BBC *Panorama* programme, a blogger noted that Ryanair was 'a cheap and popular target for any programme'.[41] In contrast to academic expectations that negative publicity and WoM may damage such brands, this particular customer seems also to have grasped the fundamental position of customer compliance businesses that such coverage is yet another piece of free advertising. Where some academics, industry commentators and the press see sensational stories and fail to grasp the essence of customer compliance management, many customers demonstrate common sense. 'Dreadful ground staff? dreadful cabin crew? humiliated passengers? Where have you seen? Not at Ryanair, in my (rather extensive) experience of that carrier,' comments one blogger;[42] while another questions the earlier noted comment of Prof. Davies by disagreeing with the professor that the company's aggressive stance would 'catch up with them'. The blogger also argues that it is much more likely that the legacy airlines will 'catch up' with O'Leary by following and adopting his business proposition. 'As we all know, humans like to spend less money and will endure much to do so. This recession is the greatest gift to him [O'Leary],' the consumer commentator concludes.

The question, though, is whether a sufficient majority of customers hold views similar to those expressed by the above mentioned bloggers. Equally important is to find out whether customer demographic and other characteristics affect the likelihood that customers will respond positively to customer compliance business practices. Academic works have linked customer attitudes towards complaining to their personality traits including 'assertiveness', 'self-confidence', general attitude towards the marketplace, 'alienation' and 'locus of control'.[43] More recently, Kanousi[44] has noted the effect that degree of masculinity or femininity has on complaints. Of interest may also be Judge et al.'s[45] notion that one's self-esteem and neuroticism affect likelihood to complain. Other studies have commented that older consumers may be more brand loyal and hence less likely to exit a relationship following a service failure. Differences have also been recorded between males and females in terms of their focus on different aspects of service failure and the differences between the two genders in experiencing complaining and in expressing emotions. We expect that effect of such traits may be weakened as far as customer compliance businesses are concerned. Even if such antecedents mattered, their influence may not be strong or consistent enough to alter substantially the standard operating procedures, scripted responses, and meticulously designed and implemented rules and regulations that customer compliance businesses use in order to manage interactions with their customers. A curious incident of the rigidity which is typical of customer compliance businesses involved Ryanair's rule that passports would be the only identity document recognised even on domestic UK flights. When socialite Tara Palmer-Tomkinson attempted to board a plane without this form of identification, she was turned back although the crew had recognised her and had asked her to sign an autograph for them.[46]

Customers' reaction to and attitudes about customer compliance practices were empirically studied by us, on four separate occasions. The general public and students were involved in research which aimed to ascertain:

1. the prevalence of various compliance practices across sectors;
2. differences between compliance businesses and traditional businesses operating in the sectors in question, in terms of the use of specific compliance practices;
3. customers' perceptions and evaluations of such practices as well as their re-patronage intentions;
4. types of practices which may be labelled customer compliance practices.

We present here only some of our findings, from a survey which was released in 2010 with the help of one of the biggest London-based market research agencies. The responses of over 1,200 customers from a sample that was representative of the general UK population were analysed. Some of them are presented in Table 7.2, in order to illustrate and support some of the points that we discuss next.

Select few of the survey results presented in Table 7.2 attest to the wide application of customer compliance practices by service providers across sectors (line A). More than 43.7 per cent of the 1,243 respondents who filled in the survey reported an incident involving their provider forcing the customer to comply with the provider's systems and processes of interaction during service recovery. Significant was also the finding that, of all sectors studied, it was in finance and banking and in electronics retail that customer compliance techniques appeared to be most widely used. Pervasive application of customer compliance techniques was also uncovered in the relations that longer-term customers build with their service providers – defined by us as customers who had been purchasing from the company for more than five years and who had made more than five purchases in the 12 months preceding the survey release. As regards this specific aspect of customer compliance, financial & banking service providers and travel businesses seem to have been applying compliance procedures more consistently and to most if not all of their customers, irrespective of the length and intensity of the relationship with these customers.

In spite of the widespread application of compliance on the part of the providers analysed in the survey, the surveyed customers did not seem deterred from using the services of the providers in question. Customers recognised the customer compliance techniques and many of them appeared to share the providers' view that there are mutual benefits from compliance management and marketing which are adequate to justify and legitimise these practices in the eyes of the providers and their customers. Although our interpretation may be contested by some academics, exemplary of 'acceptance' on the part of customers were the high readings for number (and percentage) of surveyed customers who had been subject to customer compliance procedures but who had decided not to complain (Table 7.2, line C). Equally significant was the high percentage of surveyed customers who had experienced customer compliance and who appeared undeterred from using the provider's services in the future (re-patronage) (Table 7.2, lines D and E).

Service marketing academics may argue that such readings demonstrate not so much acceptance of customer compliance practices but resignation on the part of the customers who may know that voicing concerns would achieve little, that an exit would be prohibitively costly, or that other service providers provide a similar type of treatment. In order to explore such silence and unwillingness on the part of customers to terminate their relations with customer compliance businesses, we had also organised a round of qualitative research during which 235 respondents in UK's West Midlands were interviewed on matters of service provision, satisfaction and dissatisfaction with, complaint behaviour towards, and purchase intentions towards specific low-cost airlines which are also customer compliance businesses. With the empirical findings reported elsewhere,[47] and in order to avoid unnecessary repetition, we will only briefly comment on the six interview themes uncovered during this particular phase of our research programme. The themes clearly demonstrate the high level of understanding on the part of customers of the nature and benefits of what we refer to here as customer compliance marketing. Respondents accepted the inflexible procedures, the compliance-seeking outcomes and the rigidity of interactions with customer compliance businesses. Contrary to expectations in some circles of marketing thinking, not only did these customers seem to be rewarding customer compliance businesses by not taking their custom elsewhere but many of them also recommended the companies in question, thus spreading positive WoM.

We have reproduced below only some more important findings and illustrative quotes with respect to the six themes in question.

Theme 1: Participants had positive perceptions towards the customer compliance businesses they discussed (89 per cent), and very few appeared to have been influenced by negative stories of the poor experiences of other passengers (17 per cent).

Theme 2: Interviewees gave mostly positive reviews of the customer compliance businesses in question (91 per cent), thus spreading positive WoM in networks of close relationships, mostly with friends and family members.

Theme 3: All three groups interviewed – those who had been customers and who had experienced some form of control and customer compliance, those who had not experienced control and restriction of some form, and potential customers – shared the intention to use the customer compliance businesses in question in the future.

Theme 4: A substantial majority of interviewees were undeterred by negative media coverage of the companies they analysed during the interviews. Instead of focusing on media content and coverage, the respondents reported that their perceptions, attitudes and actual behaviours were influenced by their own (often unproblematic and satisfying) experiences. Attitudes towards the customer compliance businesses were mainly positive and satisfactory. Customers agreed that, in spite of certain glitches and providers' attempts to constrict their behavioural options, the service provided and the value-for-money approach of the customer compliance businesses outweighed such negative experiences and critical press coverage. One customer noted that they 'purely couldn't care less' while another commented that 'I've heard of it being called a cattle market'.

Theme 5: Problems seemed to have involved 'others' but not the interviewees, and few close relations of the customers had experienced dissatisfaction (17 per cent). Even such stories did not appear to have the lasting negative effect anticipated in some marketing texts.

Theme 6: Participants seemed to have 'learnt' the rules of engagement with customer compliance businesses, with frequent comments that these aspects of service provision were 'to be expected'.

A final measure of acceptance of the practices of customer compliance businesses among customers and the strong position of these businesses are the statistics that we have supplied of the growing market share and large customer base of these companies – a trend which does not seem to have been majorly affected by the current economic downturn.

---

### Chapter summary for managers:

o *Customer compliance businesses have discovered a novel approach to pleasing customers which is path-breaking whereby efficiencies are being sought through the dismantling of costly supply chains and unnecessary activities.*

o *Negative attitudes towards and unfavourable portrayal of customer compliance businesses dominate in media and academic work.*

o *There seems to exist much misunderstanding about the nature, consequences and benefits of the operations of these businesses, both for their customers and society.*

o *Criticisms of customer compliance businesses fail to explain the competitive advantage of such companies over their traditional rivals.*

o *In spite of criticisms and allegations of weak service provision, customer reactions are generally positive or rational. Once customers become accustomed to compliance requirements, the majority of customers accept the low prices as well as compliance regulations.*

# 8 What the Future May Hold for Customer Compliance Businesses, their Customers and Competitors

---

**Key questions in this chapter:**

o *Has your company asked itself what the future may look like in the sector where it operates?*

o *Do you believe that companies can achieve and sustain competitive advantage and consistently beat their rivals in today's hyper-competitive high-velocity environment?*

o *Have your managers identified key solutions and competencies which your competitors may find difficult to identify or imitate?*

---

## 8.1 Clarifying the nature and benefits of compliance

This last chapter summarises some more important features of the novel business practices that we have identified and the sources of founding and growth of customer compliance companies. It also attempts to identify pointers and provides indications about the prospects of these companies and the future of their customers, the sectors and service categories where they operate, and their competitors.

As noted at the very start of this discussion, the term 'compliance' is not new to the select few marketing academics who have published on this concept or related topics. The term has appeared more consistently, in different guises, across social science disciplines. It is primarily associated with regulatory observance and ethical conformity, both of which indicate an emphasis in analyses on adherence to standards, regulations and other requirements involving, for instance, risk assessment and management as well as the fulfilment of expectations and requirements on the part of governmental regulatory bodies. In engineering, the term is used differently – to describe a body which has properties opposite to those of stiffness, hardness and inflexibility. However, throughout this book, the term has been applied in a distinct manner, denoting favourable

customer responses to requests, demands, requirements and pressures introduced by a set of technology-enabled and technology-empowered businesses
as an integral part of the novel offers of such businesses.

In spite of the substantial, consistent and frequently negative media
attention as well as the Schadenfreude – deriving pleasure from the misfor-
tunes of someone else – of some commentators that the businesses practising
compliance have attracted, the use of 'compliance', 'customer compliance
businesses' and 'customer compliance business model' in this book implies
few if any negative connotations. Unwelcome media and scholarly attention
to alleged substandard service provision of such companies may need to be
revisited. Equally important, erroneous and, at times, ill-advised academic
analyses of the principles of operation of such companies should be questioned and challenged, even if such reflective questioning invites a revisit of
fundamentals of marketing thought with respect to notions such as customer
centricity, the marketing concept, the relationship marketing concept, and
the service dominant logic thesis. We believe that these are among the main
lessons to take from this book. Although such assertions and conclusions
may be contentious, possibly divisive and potentially contestable – likely
to provoke polemical debates in some sections of marketing academia and
among practitioners – it is the authors' conviction (empirically backed by the
examples provided throughout the book) that customer compliance businesses have much to offer to the sectors where they operate and the customers they serve. Their efforts to open up service provision in a variety of
contexts have democratised the respective sectors and industries, product and
service categories which had not been widely available, had been unavailable
to consumers from certain socio-economic backgrounds, or which had been
provided as limited offers, failing to meet latent consumer needs. In return
for such democratisation, the lowered prices that customers pay for taking
advantage of new offers, and the widened set of choices available to these
customers, these businesses demand discipline and obedience on the part
of key stakeholders. Passivity is expected and exacted with respect to those
aspects of business operations which contribute much, if not most, to costs.
Although difficult customers and serial complainers may have misgivings
about customer compliance businesses, the advantage is that the majority of
customers do benefit from being compliant to prescribed business systems
and pre-set formats, such as those described in past sections.

Elements of compliance, though, are not entirely new. Manufacturers,
retailers and service providers have always required customers to observe their
regulations and comply with their procedures and rules in one way or another.
In order that customers obtain what they want, customers have to demonstrate obedience and some level of passivity not too dissimilar to that expected
by customer compliance businesses. Therefore, customer control, power application on the part of providers with their hidden commissions, and compliance have long preceded the arrival of the businesses analysed in this book.
Older generations will remember that, in order to buy an airline ticket, they
had to visit a travel agent and depend on the travel agent to explore offers and

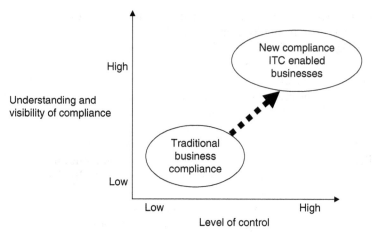

Figure 8.1   **'Old' versus 'new' customer compliance**
Source: Kasabov and Warlow (2009)

suggest solutions by using the global booking software systems. Similarly, customers had to visit brokers if they wished to buy car insurance. There, they were required to get a cover note and wait for the policy. In the area of government services, identity validation has always been a requirement (and the bureaucracy surrounding this seems to have increased in the face of terrorism and identity theft). This is, and always was, a slow process which required candidates to pass a series of steps proving their identity. The important point, one that we have also raised in an earlier publication,[1] is that compliance has always been present in customer-provider interactions. Furthermore, it will always be part of such interactions, in one form or another, because it protects companies. However, as Figure 8.1 demonstrates, there are significant differences between the type of compliance theorised here ('new' compliance) and traditional forms of company control ('old' compliance). The break of 'new' compliance from past compliance practices is in terms of it relying upon some level of customer control and of compliance becoming more visible, obvious and not hidden. As we have noted on a few occasions in the text, customer compliance systems and procedures are openly communicated by some of the companies practising them. These compliance systems and procedures also seem to be largely understood by customers.

---

### Section summary for managers:

o *The term compliance is not new, and work on this subject has appeared across social science disciplines, occasionally being analysed by marketing academics as well.*

o *In this book, the concept has been applied to contrast the innovations in service provision, research and strategising implemented by a set of highly successful businesses with traditional business models predicated on the idea of customer centricity to which many companies pay lip service.*

o *Customer compliance businesses have developed a number of services and markets to socio-economic groups who were not previously available. In return for such democratisation and widened sets of choices available to customers, these companies expect some obedience on the part of customers and other key stakeholders.*

## 8.2   Current success through customer compliance

The performance of the customer compliance businesses, discussed in this book, has been remarkable in the past two decades or so. They have achieved some form of competitive advantage over incumbents as well as other technology-enabled and web-based businesses, using a number of strategies which will be detailed below. Pricing, though not discussed in much detail in past sections of the book, has a role to play in advancing the position of these businesses. Companies tend to maximise profitability by devising and applying a number of pricing strategies which would not have been available to traditional businesses or which have been trialled and applied by customer compliance businesses or similarly entrepreneurial companies.

Some companies allow customers to decide what price they are willing to pay for a good or a service, thus matching better the value of their service offers ('Value' on Figure 8.2) with the price that the customer is charged for consuming the service. By involving customers in value creation and service provision in this manner – an example of what may be termed surface or skin-deep empowerment – the company creates the impression that the customer is in charge and may appropriate a considerably greater part of the 'consumer surplus' (denoted with ⬧), rather than 'allow' the service provider to appropriate it.

A notable example of clever pricing strategies on the part of certain customer compliance businesses is eBay, but the pricing strategy adopted by some low-cost airlines has reversed traditional airline pricing strategies of charging early bookers the highest price. Low-cost airlines sell seats at the lowest price to early bookers and increase prices as the aircraft fills (sometimes achieved by automated algorithms) closer to the flight take-off date. This results in very high load factors compared to those of traditional airlines. At times, these companies combine some of the above-mentioned pricing strategies with link marketing, thus augmenting their profits at minimal marginal cost to the business. Customers are seamlessly guided through affiliated websites where they are allegedly in control of opting for specific service features, combining such features and controlling to an

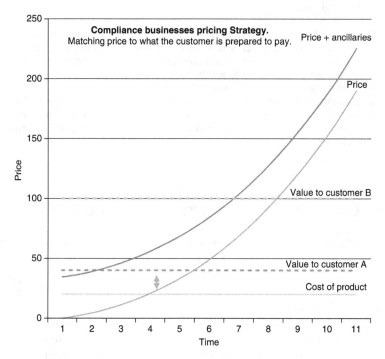

Figure 8.2   **Value creation, pricing and consumer surplus**
Adapted from Wheelan and Hunger (2002), Hunger and Wheelan (2007)

extent the price that they ultimately pay for services and service bundles. The annual accounts of both Ryanair and easyJet suggest that some customer compliance businesses would be operating at a loss, had these clever pricing and combined pricing-link marketing strategies not been adopted, whereby customers opt to purchase additional high-profit items which cost the airline nothing or very little.[2]

Examples of additional innovative pricing strategies may be found on Amazon's website. The company provides opportunities for third-party sellers to offer their products through its website at a price which is lower than what Amazon charges for goods supplied from their own warehouses. Although such a pricing strategy may appear counter-intuitive, it allows Amazon to build its customer database and control interactions between its customers and third-party suppliers, a clear example of customer compliance business control. Amazon also earns commissions from third-party sellers. The fundamental principle of this pricing strategy is that the more pieces of data that Amazon acquires on each customer, the more accurately the company can offer additional services and products that the customer may want, through automated marketing and at minimal extra effort on the part of the business. Furthermore, such pricing encourages further traffic through the company's website, thus increasing the visibility of the business, when compared to its offline competitors and online rivals. Pricing of this type empirically illustrates a crucial aspect of the business model of customer compliance businesses which we have already discussed at some length, that is, the ability of these companies to innovate in areas of value creation and value chain design by making best use of their partners[3] while also extracting maximum value from their in-house databases.[4]

Lastly, in view of the ease with which prices can be modified quickly on the Internet, customer compliance businesses alter price offers in real time, often driven by automated back-office marketing algorithms. Based on real demand and calculations of elasticity of specific markets, products and services can be priced so that they match elasticity of demand, thus improving sales and maximising profits. Such strategies appear to be particularly effective in sectors marked by highly perishable products and services such as air transport and hospitality.

Customer compliance businesses have been cultivating and perfecting a business model grounded in the design and implementation of a hybrid strategy which combines the classical business-level strategies of cost leadership (using the building block of superior efficiency), differentiation (often applying a combination of building blocks such as superior customer responsiveness, superior innovation, and superior quality) and focus (by targeting very carefully their messages at specific or niche audiences, as well as individual customers, which frequently proves to be both more effective and efficient) (see Figure 8.3) which, though introduced in Porter's[5] study of strategy types and competitive advantage, are philosophically linked to, and founded upon, Abell's 'business definition' as a rather basic and useful tool to analyse and systematise the orientation of any business. To remind ourselves, Abell described businesses and their strategic orientation with respect to customer needs, segments served by the company and the distinctive competencies, resources and technologies which the company harnesses for purposes of service provision and the satisfaction of specific needs of the specific segments that it seeks to serve.

Figure 8.3 provides the example of IKEA in order to illustrate the 'hybrid' nature of such companies as well as the role and place of hybrid strategising to their competitive success. Taking Porter's strategic option of 'cost leadership' (bottom left hand side quadrant, Figure 8.3) as the starting point of our overview, this is an option adopted by companies which seek to outcompete their competitors by controlling costs. Such control can be achieved by carefully monitoring and containing input costs (for instance, through the use of highly flexible non-unionised labour, or by taking advantage of differences in conditions across locations and national markets in terms of taxes or wage rates). Cost leadership is also frequently predicated on a business mastering experience curve effects and learning effects, whereby experience in specialised activities leads to efficiency gains for the business. Economies of

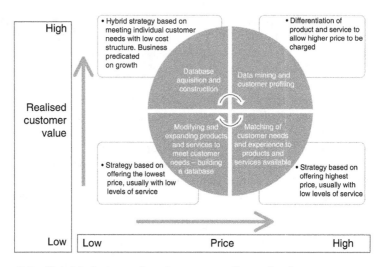

Figure 8.3  **Hybrid strategy of customer compliance businesses**
Adapted from Bowman and Faulkner (1996)

scale are pursued by re-designing company value chains, as has been shown elsewhere in our discussion.

Customer compliance businesses, though, are not pure cost leaders – a mistaken conclusion drawn by many academic commentators and one that has been criticised by us. Rather, cost leadership tends to be combined with various aspects of 'differentiation' (top right hand side quadrant, Figure 8.3), with the objective of outcompeting rivals by offering services which are perceived as unique and clearly distinguishable from rival offers.

Customer compliance businesses have thus defied the boundaries that Porter and others have traditionally drawn among the generic business-level strategies presented in the figure. That is why we find many of these companies, including IKEA, in top left hand side quadrant on Figure 8.3 – a position of innovative thinking which combines the separate spine (generic) strategies of differentiation and cost leadership into 'hybrid strategies'. Therefore, while economic operational advantages are actively sought by these companies, they are usually turned into pricing advantages for marketing purposes. Low-cost airlines – which we view as exemplary of customer compliance businesses – achieve savings by using cheaper, less crowded regional airports, flying at full capacity and ensuring fast turn-around times, using multi-tasking staff. National Bureau of Economic Research quotes that CASM (average operating costs per available seat mile, adjusted for average flight length) is around $0.10 for low-cost airlines and $0.16 for legacy airlines.

Another significant difference between customer compliance businesses and traditional rivals is that the former were among the earliest innovators

in customer relationship management by dealing directly with end customers and cutting or entirely eliminating supply chain intermediaries
such as distributors, dealers and agents. This is a particularly prominent
feature in the leisure and tourism sectors, where online booking of air and
train fares, event tickets and holidays has affected many traditional travel
companies and their high-street agents. Many of these latter types of businesses have either ceased to exist or have been forced to severely their operations. This 'novelty' in 'conducting economic exchanges' is only partly
about achieving operational effectiveness but is primarily about 'compliance' which in turn drives operational efficiency. Thus, although customer
compliance businesses provide empirical backing for Mitchell and Coles'[6]
contention that business model innovation and not technological innovation may provide lasting advantage, they also help question common
expectations in the literature that attempts on the part of entrepreneurs
to innovate business models both in terms of 'efficiency' and 'novelty'
may be 'counterproductive'. The financial position of companies that have
adopted the customer compliance business model and their growth and
dominance across sectors suggests that a 'hybrid' business model which
emphasises both 'efficiency' and 'novelty' may not only be possible but
also desirable.

A final aspect of current business success through customer compliance
concerns the moves that some customer compliance businesses have taken
to erect barriers which protect them against incumbents and likely future
competitors alike. Once a substantial barrier has been erected, customer
compliance businesses tend to lock customers in, using various means such
as easy sign-on, automatic lists of frequently bought items, volume related
discounts, low prices, high levels of service such as 'no quibble' returns,
free delivery and similar incentives to retain existing customers, especially if
these customers have shown to be capable of understanding and willing to
accept the principles of compliance. Further barriers which protect customer
compliance businesses include economic barriers predicated on economies
of scale, capital requirements, cost advantages and technological superiority.
It is sufficient to mention Amazon's substantial buying power and its successful value chain integration initiatives, including cutting out publishing
houses and dealing directly with authors. Not surprisingly, some of the biggest customer compliance businesses are currently valued in tens of billions
of dollars. Any new entrant will have to defeat a business which is not only
dominant but one which also serves its customers well, constantly innovates
and harnesses the power and superiority of its software and databases. Few
contenders would be able to match the technological superiority of customer
compliance businesses. Google's PageRank algorithm is a prime example.
Created in the 1990s at Stanford University by Brin and Page, it is widely
believed to lie at the heart of the company's success. Similarly, the power
and effective application of Amazon's and Ryanair's in-house databases are
often credited, at least partly, for the competitiveness of these two customer
compliance businesses.

> **Section summary for managers:**
>
> o *The financial performance of customer compliance businesses has been remarkable during the past two decades.*
> o *These companies have achieved, and some have sustained, competitive advantage.*
> o *Most customer compliance businesses practise some form of controlling pricing, often automatically and based on demand, so that the price charged to each individual customer matches individual demand.*
> o *Link marketing and extensively collaborating with business partners contribute to the competitive success of many customer compliance businesses.*

## 8.3   Sustainable or temporary competitive advantage through customer compliance

At the heart of strategy and marketing theories is the concept of competitive advantage,[7] founded traditionally upon an understanding of accumulation and combining of organisational resources to produce goods or services more efficiently than one's competitors.[8] Definitions of competitive advantage abound, yet the term and discussions about it are described as complicated and vague. There is no consensus about what competitiveness means and how it can be measured. Besanko, Dranove and Shanley[9] offer a simple definition which we use here to illustrate an important point about customer compliance businesses. Competitive advantage and, therefore, competitiveness are treated by Besanko and collaborators as a situation where a company outperforms rivals in its industry. Such a definition is intuitively appealing; however, it too suffers from alleged 'imprecisions' associated with alternative definitions. Furthermore, it shed no light on the understanding of 'sustained' and the role that it plays in achieving and holding on to such an advantage. Porter's (1985) earlier attempt to resolve this latter issue was equally ambiguous, when he defined sustained competitive advantage in terms of 'above average performance in the long run' (p. 11). While such a perspective is useful, in that it draws attention to the fact that only some forms of competitive advantage may be less imitable and can thus produce superior economic performance which persists, it offers few suggestions about distinctions between 'sustained' and 'non-sustained' and the ingredients of both types of advantage.

More recent attempts to clarify the meaning of 'competitive advantage' and 'sustained competitive advantage' include Wiggins and Ruefli's[10] work which builds upon and extends Porter's early thinking. Competitive advantage is defined by them with reference to the above-average company performance and the specific strategic group or industry where a company operates. The degree of sustainability of above average performance, they maintain, is always determined by current industry specific variables, with product life cycles being one such variable.

Whatever differences there are in conceptualising competitive advantage, theories about competitiveness share a common assumption that competitive advantage exists and that it is attainable,[11] based on Porter's early thinking and his generic strategies reviewed earlier in this chapter. However, more recent academic accounts, including the above-mentioned article by Wiggins and Ruefli, question the existence of competitive advantage, or at least challenge its presence in its purer form – sustained competitive advantage. To them and other theorists, sustained competitive advantage is increasingly rare. On those few occasions when the analyst comes across examples of such advantage, they maintain, it is usually of declining persistence. These assertions are backed by empirical evidence of increasingly volatile financial returns that most companies report these days, supporting an emerging consensus that the notion of sustained competitive advantage may be applicable to stable economic environments only.[12]

This shift in thinking about competitiveness has been brought about by dramatic changes, some of which have – ironically – accelerated the growth of customer compliance businesses. Technological breakthroughs and globalisation, D'Aveni[13] theorised, have progressively driven the business world towards hypercompetition, with an increased emphasis on innovation.[14] Technological breakthroughs have shortened product life-cycles, and patents have become less useful as barriers to entry that protect new technology, products and service offers. Time to market has shortened, and innovations are produced and released much more quickly. Similarly, globalisation has disrupted established patterns of competition and strategising, in the process of doing so affecting local markets. The 'new competitive landscape' is described variably, but conceptualisations tend to include references to 'high velocity markets', 'hypercompetition' and 'intense competitive actions'.[15] To these one should add the impact that the so-called Information age has had on companies and the approaches that they choose to implement, to ensure their survival and prosperity. The Internet has increased the pace of technological development and has additionally shortened the earlier mentioned product life-cycles, making products obsolete more rapidly. The Internet and other technological developments discussed in this book have reinforced the effects of globalisation by facilitating access to markets on a global scale and at a low cost. As a result, the value of traditional strategic assets that companies possess has been reduced.

One major consequence of such dramatic recent changes in competitive circumstances has been the swing in thinking about competitiveness and competitive advantage. Some commentators have come to view sustainable competitive advantage as rare or, at least, declining in duration, further increasing volatility in the business world and positively contributing to the hypercompetitive nature of many global and domestic markets.[16] It is suggested that we live in an age when companies find it difficult to manage the disorder, disequilibrium and uncertainty in external environments and when time frames of strategic actions are being reduced. Therefore, analysts such as D'Aveni view the achievement of sustainable competitive advantage as an impossible business aim. All managers can do, in the face of successive challenges, is to maintain a balance between stability in strategic planning and instability through adaptation to such external change.[17] This thesis has more recently been developed by Wiggins and Ruefli, who note that company success should be measured in terms of the ability of a business to achieve a series of temporary advantages over time.[18] Being competitive does not denote lasting superior performance. Rather, it increasingly suggests that successful businesses are those that are flexible, innovative, unpredictable, surprising their competitors by constantly searching for and exploiting opportunities in an attempt to fashion futures which they see as desirable. This is precisely what Lengnick-Hall and Wolff[19] meant by the 'strategic logic' these days being that of 'opportunity'.

Our thinking about customer compliance businesses is a logical continuation of, but also represents, discontinuity as regards current strands of thinking in strategy and marketing strategy. Firstly, we do not seek to explain sustained competitive advantage, especially over the long term. Rather, we agree with commentators such as Wiggins and Ruefli[20] and Thomas and D'Aveni[21] that advantage is increasingly temporary at best, and that it usually assumes the format of a series of temporary competitive advantages which can be achieved only through relentless innovation and opportunity search. Secondly, in writing this book, we hoped to present a framework which not only describes but also explains why some businesses these days have demonstrated the possibility of achieving such a series of temporary competitive advantages, through invention and self-reorganisation. We have referred to them as customer compliance businesses. Thirdly, ours has been a contingent view of competitiveness, for we conceptualise temporariness not only in chronological but also in sectoral and national terms.

An additional aspect of the sustainability of the philosophy, strategies and tactics of customer compliance businesses concerns the inability of their rivals, such as traditional companies operating in sectors where customer compliance businesses operate, to emulate elements of the customer compliance business model. Past attempts to replicate customer compliance include BA and KLM founding Go and Buzz, respectively. However, many of these attempts have failed, at least in the early years, suggesting that strategies and business models cannot be easily replicated. The failure of many initiatives by incumbents in the sectors 'devastated' by customer compliance businesses can be attributed to the tendency of incumbents to replicate only individual parts of the strategies of their more successful competitors – something which is easily done but which is insufficient to ensure the success of such replication initiatives. It has proven difficult to keep pace with customer compliance businesses, for they are among the few businesses demonstrating an ability to rapidly change, often automatically and in real-time, driven by algorithms in their control software. Organisational change and reinvention are difficult, not least because organisations and their managers are trained to sustain stability and maintain those management systems and decisions that have contributed to past company success. While change, and not stability, is the norm and is expected from excellent organisations, few managers of traditional businesses have managed to pay more than lip serve to this truism.

More recent attempts to form customer compliance businesses as off-shoots of traditional companies have usually been constrained by inherited thinking on the part of the parent company, even though most attempts in question were set up as separate business entities. The inability of traditional companies to imitate the thinking and actions of customer compliance businesses has much to do with 'path dependent' resource and strategy commitments as well as thinking which inhibits traditional businesses. As a result, many incumbents have lost ground to customer compliance businesses, as has been documented throughout the book. They have been blighted by business models not conducive to change, corporate structures inhibiting innovation, and inward looking management which does not reward creativity. Whereas resource-based-view scholars contend that path dependence may assist competition through accumulating and harnessing resources,[22] customer compliance businesses demonstrate that path dependence may place considerable pressures on company fortunes and may even endanger organisational survival. Strongly path dependent thinking, rule- and regulation-related rigidities and internal politics within established players thwarted their 'ability to change'.[23] This offers a clear distinction from the relentless innovation on the part of many customer compliance businesses, in support of views that continuous improvement is key to business model effectiveness[24] and performance.[25] In conclusion, while we agree with Mitchell and Coles[26] in principle that 'industry leaders' may generate business model innovations, we believe that the arrival of customer compliance businesses marks a reversal of the trend discussed by Mitchell and Coles. Business model change and innovation have originated not in the 'industry leaders' identified by Mitchell and Coles or traditional businesses but in newcomers practising customer compliance.

A last comment on competitiveness concerns explanations of the success of at least some customer compliance businesses in terms of their 'fitness' to current economic conditions. Some commentators have pointed out that the companies that we refer to as customer compliance businesses have been assisted by the dramatic recessions of 2000 and 2008–9 – possibly backed by O'Leary's comment, 'We like a good old recession every now and then.'[27] These two dates mark major changes to which many incumbents failed to adapt. Those that adapted got a head start and captured large markets globally, making it difficult for others to catch up. Although our argument may be disputed by some, there is evidence of the success of customer compliance businesses after 2000 and of the concurrent retreat of many traditional businesses attempting to protect their position in sectors affected by customer compliance. Such empirics-based arguments provide a strong support for Morris, Schindehutte and Allen's[28] test of business models in terms of their internal and external 'fitness'. Perhaps it is this strong dual fit which is another source of competitive strength of this new innovative business model and the companies that have implemented it. Internally, the 'fit' is most aptly illustrated by the centrality of the 'compliance' theme to compliance innovations, whereas externally, customer compliance businesses have shown both coherence with external conditions and ability to flexibly change with, and align to, altering conditions. Not only do customer compliance businesses seem to be constantly engaged in looking for and adopting new strengths to generate value, but they also accomplish this during very short time periods, disproving yet another commonly accepted wisdom among researchers, based on studies of traditional businesses, that resource endowments may be changed only over the long term.

---

### Section summary for managers:

o *The rise and sustained growth of customer compliance businesses should renew academic and practitioner interest in questions of attaining and sustaining competitive advantage.*

o *The issue of whether the current advantage of many customer compliance businesses is sustainable remains to be addressed conceptually and empirically.*

o *Questions also remain regarding the ability of other companies to emulate the operations of customer compliance businesses, since many traditional businesses that have tried to copy compliance strategies and tactics have withdrawn or sold out.*

---

## 8.4   Can all customer compliance businesses be successful?

It should be clear by now that, to us, many customer compliance businesses have attained competitive advantage, growing their respective markets and pressuring incumbents. While many other companies have attempted to use the Internet and other new technologies to develop their business propositions, quite a few have suffered due to poorly designed or inadequately implemented strategies and fulfilment methods. The dot.com bubble crash witnessed mass exits, especially by businesses that had decided to compete on the basis of low price only and had ignored the dangers of the low barriers to entry of the Internet economy. Unlike them, successful customer compliance businesses consistently added value and avoided competing on the basis of selling below cost, as many of the failed companies did. Brands such as IKEA, Ryanair and financial service providers expanded the use of database marketing and, subsequently, automated marketing. Their growth has been remarkable. eBay increased its gross merchandise volume by 17 per cent in 2006 alone. Since 1995 it had attracted over 250 million customers.[29] Other customer compliance businesses such as Amazon and Southwest Airlines are frequently noted for their 'market driving' innovations.[30] We have identified the ingredients and consequences of the business model innovations introduced by these businesses, and demonstrated the difficulty in imitating or even conceptualising this business model. It is different from the e-business models described in the literature and has radically departed from the earlier dot.com models, many of which were predicated mainly on pricing and technology application. Its uniqueness in terms of combining hybrid, market-driving thinking, democratised processes, collaborations with partners and competitors, innovative relations with customers and radically re-designed service provision has proved hard to theorise and even harder to replicate.

Such a discussion of customer compliance may have left the reader with the impression that all such companies have been, and are, successful. This is obviously not the case, as some customer compliance businesses have failed. In fact, the vast majority of new start-up businesses predicated on novel technologies fail or tend to remain niche e-commerce players.

We should apologise at this point, for explanations and examples of business success only through customer compliance were provided by us, at the expense of the analysis of failure, its sources and consequences. However, this discussion was initially commissioned and, therefore, designed as a testament to the 'success' of novel practitioner recipes which help set some companies apart from others. It was always going to be a snapshot of technology-enabled accomplishment and triumph in the face of adversity. A combined investigation of success and failure, as well as of their separate sources and very distinct effects, is beyond the scope of this book. The proper investigation of failure, though instructive and hence of interest to practitioner and scholarly audiences alike, would require a separate manuscript of comparable length and complexity.

Future studies of customer compliance, though, are invited, to reveal the complexities of failure, by identifying cases of customer compliance failure. The conditions under which this business model is likely to remain competitive should also be explored. Based on our belief that these companies seem to 'fit' current market conditions and the changes taking place following the information revolution, future environmental transformations may eventually weaken these businesses. Such a scenario should be properly theorised. The question of 'manipulating' or creating conditions such as those that favour customer compliance businesses also warrants scholarly attention.

Any future analysis should avoid confusing, and equating, customer compliance businesses with dot.coms. As the preceding chapters have demonstrated, customer compliance businesses are not necessarily pure dot.com companies. Although their success is often attributed to their superior application of database marketing, automated marketing and new technologies, including those used for purposes of automated market and marketing research, they are a category of companies which clearly stand out in terms of their underlying business logic, which is a considerably more central aspect of their operation than technology solutions per se.

---

**Section summary for managers:**

o *Customer compliance businesses are distinct from, and should not be confused with, dot.com businesses.*

o *Although being enabled by new technologies, customer compliance businesses primarily create value through database and automated marketing.*

o *Not all customer compliance businesses have been successful, and the majority of start-ups fail. In this book, we have reviewed only successful customer compliance businesses and explored the opportunities for benchmarking by applying best practice as part of compliance.*

o *Further studies are required to identify the ingredients of sustaining competitive advantage through customer compliance.*

---

## 8.5    Is customer compliance applicable outside the private sector and to developed economies?

There are fundamental differences in the adoption of information technology in the public and private sectors. The public sector appears much more cautious and conservative in its response to the arrival of some technologies documented by us. Coupled with bureaucratic planning processes, path dependent norms and entrenched attitudes, including the protection of jobs and hierarchies by senior civil servants, this tends to inhibit innovation in the way that it has occurred in the private sector in the past two decades. Most of the software and other technological tools supplied to the public sector have been developed by private sector companies, to specifications defined by civil servants. Typically these are attempts to computerise existing manual systems rather than redesign systems and organisational mentalities, as has been the case with customer compliance businesses. Specifications, tendering processes and contracts are frequently drawn up by senior public sector managers who may not possess sufficient understanding of what is possible, nor have the political will to introduce radical change in the way that the entrepreneurs who set up private sectors customer compliance businesses have done.

According to Prof. Kawalek from Manchester Business School, poor project governance tends to explain at least some of the performance difficulties in installing IT systems in the public sector. However, quite often these projects are not ICT projects at all, but are change initiatives or transformation projects that have, at their heart, what Kawalek refers to as 'destructive technology'. The aim of destroying 'old ways of doing business' is central to customer compliance businesses' innovations in the private sector. Many of these companies started by identifying a need, developing a strategy to meet that need, and only then designing software or applying technologies suited to the achievement of very specific strategic goals and a business vision (of customer compliance). If the implementation of such initiatives involved destroying traditional business strategies or whole business sectors in order to gain a competitive advantage, these were viewed as painful yet necessary outcomes of renewal and innovativeness. Achieving the same results and applying the same or a similar logic in the public sector would prove taxing – complications of political, cultural, organisational and social nature are likely to thwart any efforts to deliberately destroy established systems and thinking.

The above comments may be considered more applicable to large projects, including the GBP 12.7 bn computerisation of UK's National Health Service which was cancelled by the Conservative-Liberal Democrat government in September 2010. Application of call-centre technology, use of websites to provide information, FAQs (frequently asked questions) have all proved effective in reducing the demand for face-to-face communication between government services and departments and the general public. Nevertheless, and in spite of the number of recent high-profile failures of public sector IT projects not only in the UK but also elsewhere, as well as growing pressures for e-government as a fundamental change to public sector culture, the application of customer compliance philosophy is not a strategy which fits well with bureaucratic and political ways of making decisions. Individual elements of customer compliance have been noted by us in the process of preparing materials for this book, including recent calls in the UK public sector to employ 'customer disengagement' tactics such as those used by HM Revenue & Customs. However, uncovering and therefore researching systemic-type compliance in public sector services would be complex and are yet to come.

As regards the applicability of the analysis to less developed and emerging economies, the origins of customer compliance thinking are clearly found in company practices in Europe and USA. The most striking examples of customer compliance – in terms of their innovativeness and effect on customers, incumbents and society – are also found in these economies. In light of such concentration of customer compliance thinking in the 'developed West', our analysis has focused on the European and US experiences, at the expense of the study of similar developments elsewhere in the world which, to our knowledge, have not been reported sufficiently well in order to ascertain their belonging to the set of customer compliance practices. As a piece of analysis aimed primarily at a practitioner audience, it has also been a book aiming to converse with, and persuade, practitioners in Europe and the USA of the validity of customer compliance and of the possibility that such a novel philosophy offers, not the least in terms of benchmarking their business practices against those described by us here.

The dominance of European and US companies in the set of companies defined as customer compliance businesses may also be attributed to cultural characteristics of customers and managers in those environments;

however, the level of development of service sectors in the BRIC (Brazil, Russia, India, China) countries is rapid, with call-centre technology at times surpassing changes in the developed countries. The Internet and modern satellite enabled telephony have allowed knowledge-based activities, particularly in the IT sector, to be undertaken off-shore in these lower wage economies. These markets have large pools of well-educated workers, specifically with skills in IT and software production operating with production costs which are a fraction of those in the Western economies. Business Process Outsourcing (BPO) organisations typical of the sort of companies involved in India's USD 47 bn BPO sector are Tata Consultancy Services Ltd, Infosys Technologies Ltd, Wipro Technologies and HCL Technologies Ltd. It should not be assumed that these are poor relations or subcontractors of companies in the developed world, for many have turned into active producers themselves of software which is new and innovative and which is increasingly used by customer compliance businesses.

BPO services have attracted attention to the value of education to BRIC countries by offering solutions to trade-related displacements. In spite of potential implications such as the erosion of comparative advantage of high-wage nations, we should not forget that the technologies and solutions analysed in this book, as well as the whole digital economy, still tend to be rather unevenly distributed. Such unevenness explains, and shapes, the way in which technology-driven business opportunities and economic developments such as customer compliance tend to occur and spread.

---

### Section summary for managers:

o *The public sector is showing reluctance to acknowledge the adoption of customer compliance strategies, though elements of customer compliance are readily identifiable.*

o *Developing countries lag behind the developed West in terms of nurturing customer compliance businesses. However, B2B companies such as Indian engineering and IT firms are active in developing and supplying call-centre and other technology solutions which are key to customer compliance operations.*

---

## 8.6   The future place of compliance in marketing thought

In the search for explanations of the nature and sources of customer compliance success, we aimed to communicate our views to practitioners. Although overviews of, and references to, marketing theory were consciously minimised, classics and more recent views in the discipline had to be incorporated, to form the conceptual basis of our discussion. Since the thesis of the book questions much of what is currently advocated in streams of academic thinking in marketing and especially in some studies of service provision, reminders about the precepts of such thinking were required, not least in order to accentuate the novelty of the marketing practices discussed here. This book sought to highlight the 'common denominators' among diverse businesses and their practices which, at first glance, may appear too distinct to belong to the same family or category of similar entities. Although significant differences exist among customer compliance businesses with respect to their operation, there are also sufficient commonalities – in terms of their adoption of 'compliance' – that affect various aspects of their business and may reveal opportunities for future developments in sectors which have not been affected by customer compliance yet.

In spite of the practitioner orientation of this discussion, we feel that it is appropriate to end it with a brief reminder of what customer compliance has to offer to marketing thought. Equally importantly, of interest to us is not only whether marketing academics become receptive to potentially heretical ideas but also how, and if, these new business practices will, or may, be taught by academics to future generations of marketing and strategy students. As noted elsewhere in the discussion, marketing theory has remained captivated by the twin notions of 'customer centricity' and 'marketing orientation' for too long. Waves of researchers have remained faithful to dictums of customer needs and wants forming the basis of decision making and strategising. Such thinking has been rarely questioned by mainstream academics in our discipline. In fact, normative marketing discourses have recently become more, and not less, intrigued by such issues and have not attempted to explore different solutions to the question of customer needs and pleasing customers. This is evidenced not only by the relatively recent arrival of relationship marketing thinking but also by the current dominance of concepts such as 'service dominant logic' and 'loving' customers. These new additions to age-old theses, rhetoric and dominant marketing imaginaries are even more emphatic about the role, place and importance of customer centricity to marketing thinking and practice. As a result, the number and variety of articles in current mainstream marketing thought which tackle various aspects of relationship marketing initiatives, customer-oriented programmes, and customer relationship management seem to be growing, with few voices offering alternative solutions and answers, let alone posing unorthodox questions.

By reviewing practitioners' and academics' work on customer centricity, market and customer orientation and related matters, and also by empirically and conceptually presenting a different approach to strategising and managing relations with customers and other important stakeholder groups, we hoped to raise the prominence of questions which, we believe, are critical to the future maturation and development of marketing – especially if it wishes to gain 'academic respectability' and alter its 'lowly standing in a scholarly caste system'.[31] Firstly, we were curious, prior to starting working on this book and the conceptual and empirical research on customer compliance which preceded it, whether concepts such as 'customer centricity' made sense economically, that is, if it cost more to businesses than it delivered in terms of added customer value and profits. Secondly, we wanted to explore whether businesses *actually* practised such 'customer centricity' or merely paid lip service to it, or completely ignored it in favour of alternative ways of managing relations and attaining competiveness. Lastly, there was the issue of whether the expectations and needs of customers were actually correctly identified by proponents of 'customer centricity' or whether customer needs are being better met using a different business philosophy. We still find these questions intellectually stimulating, and hope that the answers we have provided will be of use to practitioners and the academics who instruct them as students and shape them in their formative years.

---

### *Book summary for managers:*

o *This book searched for an explanation of the strengths, sources of success and the future of an innovative set of companies termed customer compliance businesses.*

o *Our discussion questioned notions central to marketing theory, such as customer centricity, by revealing the ability of customer compliance businesses to please their customer better than traditional businesses purporting to practise customer centricity.*

o *We identified common practices among a diverse and rapidly developing set of companies.*

o *The book attempted to raise thought-provoking issues about the current state of marketing, service provision and strategy as well as future developments in practice and theory in both disciplines. While certain aspects of our thinking may appear heretical to some, we trust that our explanation offers an improved understanding of highly successful business practices across sectors.*

# Notes

## 1 Defining and Understanding Customer Compliance

1. For instance Glass, McKillop and Rasaratnam 2010; Inderst 2010.
2. van Dijke and Verboon 2010.
3. Masters 2010.
4. Ko, Mendeloff and Gray 2010.
5. Sam 2010.
6. Hibbs and Piculescu 2010.
7. Avdeyeva 2010.
8. Douglas and Berendien 2010; Nijsen et al. 2009.
9. Hausman and Johnston 2010.
10. E.g., Scott 2008.
11. Tudhope, Prinsloo and Pitt 2007; Stegman 2008.
12. 2009.
13. Dellande, Gilly and Graham 2004; Dellande and Nyer 2007.
14. See Humphreys 2006; Kasabov 2007; Shankar, Cherrier and Canniford 2006; Zwick and Dholakia 2004a, 2004b.

## 2 How Did it All Come About?

1. Robinson 2000.
2. Dyck and Reinbergs 1998.
3. Quader 2007.
4. McCosker 2003; Warrier 2007.
5. Lindgreen, Palmer and Vanhamme 2004.
6. Robinson 2000.
7. Fawcett and Farris 1998.
8. Button 2003.
9. Button and Nijkamp 2003.
10. Domanico 2007.
11. 2000.
12. Quader 2007.
13. Goss 1995.
14. Berry and Linoff 2000; Rud 2001.
15. Vriens and Grigsby 2001.
16. Fayyad 2001.

17. Box and Texas 2005.
18. E.g. Malone, Yates and Benjamin 1987.
19. Warrier 2007.
20. McCosker 2003.
21. Spencer-Matthews and Lawley 2006.
22. See Day 2000.
23. Henderson and Murray 2005.

## 3   The Technology and its Applications

1. 2006
2. See also Colgate and Danaher 2000.
3. Day 2000.
4. Goodman 1992; Labe 1994.
5. Reid and Catterall 2005.
6. 2006.
7. 2005.
8. Chen and Chen 2004; Jackson 2007.
9. 2006.
10. Reuters, 2011; http://www.reuters.com/article/2011/10/03/us-hp-autonomy-idUSTRE79269E20111003.
11. 2006.
12. 2006.
13. Tapp and Hughes 2004.
14. Adam, Vocino and Bednall. 2009.
15. Sayer 2005.
16. Morris and Feldman 1997.
17. Macdonald and Sirianni 1996; Batt and Moynihan 2002.
18. Taylor and Bain 1999; Callaghan and Thompson 2001.
19. 2004.
20. 2007.
21. Callaghan and Thompson 2001.
22. Fernie and Metcalf 1998.
23. See Buhalis 2004.
24. Varadarajan and Yadav 2002.
25. Brookes and Palmer 2003.
26. Brennan, Baines and Garneau 2003.
27. Smith et al. 2001.
28. Lindgreen, Palmer and Vanhamme 2004.
29. Coad 2006.
30. E.g. Oliver 1997; Szymanski and Henard 2001.
31. See Turban, Rainer and Potter 2001, Turban et al. 2002.

## 4   New Forms of Service Provision

1. McKitterick 1957.
2. 1954.

3. 1959.
4. 1972.
5. E.g., 1990.
6. Brady and Cronin 2001.
7. Narver and Slater 1990.
8. Addis and Podesta 2005.
9. Lindgreen, Palmer and Vanhamme 2004.
10. Mitussis, O'Malley and Patterson 2006.
11. E.g., Ford 1990; Mattson 1997.
12. Gummesson 1999.
13. Jaworski and Kohli 1993; Greenley et al. 2004.
14. 2004.
15. Zeithaml, Parasuraman and Berry 1985.
16. 1985.
17. Parasuraman, Zeithaml and Berry 1988.
18. Sureshchandar, Rajendran and Anantharaman 2002.
19. Dean and Terziovski 2000; Spencer-Matthews and Lawley 2006.
20. Spencer-Matthews and Lawley 2006.
21. Gilmore 2001.
22. Maxham 2001.
23. Johnston and Clark 2005.
24. Kelley, Hoffman and Davis 1993.
25. McCollough, Berry and Yadav 2000.
26. McCollough, Berry and Yadav 2000.
27. Wirtz and Mattila 2004.
28. Weun, Beatty and Jones 2004.
29. See Kasabov 2010; Kasabov and Warlow 2009.
30. Kasabov 2004.
31. Baer and Hill 1994; Smart and Martin 1992.
32. Kasabov 2010.
33. Beatty and Smith 1987; Gruen, Summers and Acito 2000.
34. Autry, Hill and O'Brien 2007.
35. Steinauer 1997; Tomlinson 2002.
36. 2004.
37. 2006.
38. 1999.
39. 2006.
40. Bell, Menguc and Stefani 2004.
41. 2010.
42. 2005.
43. 1999.
44. Humphrey and Ashforth 1994.
45. Newing 2007.
46. Reisch 2001; Rha and Widdows 2002; Urban 2003.
47. 2000 and 2004.
48. Prahalad and Ramaswamy 2004.
49. 1996.

50. 2008.
51. Anitsal and Schumann 2007.
52. 2000.
53. 2006.
54. 2006.
55. 2001.
56. 2000.
57. Lusch and Vargo 2006.
58. Vargo and Lusch 2004.
59. Frow and Payne 2007.
60. Ballantyne and Varey 2008.
61. Payne, Store Acka and Frow 2008.
62. 2005.
63. 2006.
64. 2006.
65. 2008.
66. p. 355.
67. p. 359.
68. 2004a, 2004b.
69. 2008.
70. 1997.
71. 2006.
72. See also Horkheimer and Adorno 1944.
73. Singh and Wilkes 1996.
74. Shaw 2007.
75. Seyfang 2007.
76. See Smith 2006.
77. Alleyne 2005.
78. http://www.i-hate-ikea.org/.
79. www.facebook.com/ikea.attack.
80. 2012. http://www.guardian.co.uk/business/2012/mar/14/ikea-accused-detectives-customers-france.
81. Hodgson 2002; Schroter 1997; Skalen, Fellesson and Fougere 2006.
82. See Liljander and Roos 2002.
83. Olsen and Johnson 2003.
84. 2003.
85. 2003.
86. Dowling and Staelin 1994.
87. Jarvenpaa and Tractinsky 2000.
88. Keen et al. 2004.
89. 2002.
90. See Stockdale 2007.
91. Palmer, Beggs and McMullan 2000.
92. Degeratu, Rangaswamy and Wu 2000.
93. Riegelsberger, Sasse and McCarthy 2003.

94. Johnson and Grayson 2005.
95. Aikena et al. 2008.
96. 1999.
97. 2000.
98. 2000.
99. 1999.
100. 2008.
101. Helm 2004.
102. Chylinski and Chu 2010.

# 5 Automated Market and Marketing Research

1. Kotler 2000.
2. Burns and Bush 2003.
3. Brookes and Palmer 2003.
4. Palmer 2004.
5. Kasouf, Celuch and Strieter 1995; Naylor 2003.
6. 1997.
7. 2003.
8. 1995.
9. 2008.
10. Kasabov 2010; Kasabov and Warlow 2009.
11. Kotler and Keller 2006.
12. Kotler and Keller 2006.
13. Schoenbachler et al. 1997.
14. Tomlinson and Evans 2005.
15. Collinson 2001.
16. Haig 2004.
17. Fiore 2001; Strauss and Frost 2001.
18. Haig 2004.
19. See Brennan, Baines and Garneau 2008.
20. Smith et al. 2001.
21. Coad 2006.
22. Epsilon 2007.
23. Lindgreen, Palmer and Vanhamme 2004.
24. Grönroos 1990, 1995.
25. Datamonitor 2007.
26. See also Alreck and Settle 2007.
27. 2007.
28. Campanelli 2006; Kadet 2006; Turow, Feldman and Meltzer 2005.
29. Singh and Singh 2008.
30. Pitta and Fowler 2005.
31. King 2008.
32. Wyner 2008.
33. See also McWilliam 2000.

34. Epsilon 2007.
35. Zakon 2005.
36. See Hair et al. 2007.

# 6   Innovations in Business Model and Strategy

1. Morris, Schindehutte and Allen 2005.
2. Amit and Zott 2001.
3. Chesbrough and Rosenbloom 2002.
4. Magretta 2002; Shin and Park 2009.
5. 2003.
6. 2002.
7. 2003.
8. Amit and Zott 2001; Zott and Amit 2007, 2008.
9. Mahadevan 2000.
10. Afuah and Tucci 2001.
11. Alt and Zimmermann 2001.
12. Weill and Vitale 2001.
13. 2003.
14. Kim, Nam and Stimpert 2004.
15. 2000.
16. 2001.
17. Buhalis 2004.
18. Ryanair press release, 21 August 2007.
19. Robertson 2010.
20. Brady and Norris 2009.
21. Rungtusanatham et al. 2003.
22. Zott, Amit and Donlevy 2000.
23. IdeaWorks, 2008; http://www.ideaworkscompany.com/press/021908
    AnalysisRyanairAncillary2008.pdf; Ryanair's ancillary revenues after
    2007 have grown, and the income derived from ancillary sales is pub-
    lished in the company's annual reports – see Ryanair, 2011; http://www.
    ryanair.com/doc/investor/2011/Annual_Report_2011_Final.pdf.
24. Meyer 1982; Nonaka 1994.
25. Arnold 2002.
26. 2006.
27. Radhika 2003.
28. Edvardsson and Enquist, 2009.
29. Insert    http://www.ikea.com/ms/en_US/jobs/join_us/ikea_values/
    index.html#.
30. http://franchisor.ikea.com/showContent.asp?swfld.
31. Reichert, 1998.
32. http://www.ikeafamilylive.com/en/room/express-yourself-845.
33. See Hollingshead, 2005.
34. Creaton 2007.

35. Johnson 2006.
36. Carrillat, Jaramillo and Locander 2004.
37. Henkel et al. 2007.
38. Johnson 2006.
39. Darling et al. 2007.
40. Rodgriguez 2012.
41. http://www.youtube.com/watch?v=KYRHMckJPhU.
42. http://www.youtube.com/watch?v=UfIY24BErBE.
43. Mascarenhas, *Kesavan* and *Bernacchi* 2004.
44. Warrier, 2007; Webanalytics, 2008.
45. Sonpal 2006; Wall Street Journal 2011.
46. Grol and Schoch 1998, p. 3.
47. *The Guardian*, 12 October 2002.
48. Domanico 2007.
49. Proff 2000.
50. Carrillat, Jaramillo and Locander 2004.
51. Rust and Chung 2006.
52. Meuter et al. 2000.
53. Amit and Zott 2001.

# 7 Reactions to Customer Compliance Businesses

1. Boshoff 1997.
2. Dick and Basu 1994.
3. 2004.
4. Maxham 2001.
5. Hennig-Thurau et al. 2004, p. 39.
6. Kozinets 2002.
7. 2004.
8. Brown and Reingen 1987; Godes and Mayzlin 2004.
9. Arndt 1967; Silverman 1997.
10. See BBC, 1997; Verma, 2005; Bartlett, 2006; Environmental Investigation Agency 2007.
11. See Cirillo, 2011.
12. See IKEA, 2011.
13. UNICEF: http://www.unicef.org/india/partners_5198.htm.
14. Source: http://www.ikea.com/ms/en_US/about_ikea/our_responsibility/working_conditions/preventing_child_labour.html.
15. Source: http://www.ikea.com/ms/fr_FR/about_ikea/pdf/IWAY_preventing_child_labour.pdf.
16. BBC 2005.
17. BBC 2005.
18. BBC 2004.
19. BBC 2005.
20. cnn.com 2005.

21. Source:       http://www.thesun.co.uk/sol/homepage/news/101943/
    Riot-at-new-Ikea-store.html?print=yes.
22. Shipman 2007.
23. Kramer 2010.
24. See Fletcher 2007.
25. See BBC 2011; Healy 2010; Yiannopoulos, 2009; http://www.
    euronewsweek.com/2012/02/15/ryanair-in-sexist-ads-criticism/.
26. Daily Mail 2012.
27. Hough 2011.
28. BBC 2012; Daily Mail 2012.
29. BBC 2010.
30. BBC Watchdog 2008.
31. Irish Times 2010.
32. 2007.
33. 2007.
34. Schroeder and Salzer-Morling 2006.
35. 2004.
36. 2006.
37. Charitou and Markides 2003.
38. 2004.
39. http://www.pprune.org/archive/index.php/t-391756.html.
40. http://pprune.org/passengers-slf-self-loading-freight/391756-
    panorama-bbc1-monday-12th-oct-why-hate-ryanair.html.
41. http://www.pprune.org/archive/index.php/t-391756.html.
42. Source:       http://www.pprune.org/passengers-slf-self-loading-freight/
    391756-panorama-bbc1-monday-12th-oct-why-hate-ryanair.html.
43. Judge et al. 2002; Singh and Wilkes 1996.
44. 2005.
45. 2002.
46. Creaton 2007.
47. Kasabov and Warlow 2009.

# 8   What the Future May Hold for Customer Compliance Businesses, their Customers and Competitors

1. Kasabov and Warlow 2009.
2. EasyJet 2011; Ryanair 2011. Available at: http://www.ryanair.com/doc/
   investor/2011/q4_2011_doc.pdf;        http://2011annualreport.easyjet.
   com/downloads/PDFs/Full_Annual_Report_2011.pdf.
3. Mehta 2008; Sebastiao and Golicic 2008.
4. See also Deschamps 2005.
5. 1980.
6. 2003.
7. Sirmon et al. 2010.
8. Rumelt, Schendel and Teece 1994.

9. 1996.
10. 2002.
11. Rumelt et al. 1994.
12. Senior and Fleming 2006.
13. 1995.
14. Hitt, Keats and DeMarie (1998).
15. See Ilinitch, D'Aveni and Lewin 1996.
16. D'Aveni, Dagnino and Smith 2010.
17. Thiétart and Forgues 1995.
18. Thomas and D'Aveni 2009; Wiggins and Ruefli 2005.
19. 1999.
20. 2005.
21. 2009.
22. Wilk and Fensterseifer 2003.
23. Lawler and Worley 2006.
24. Mitchell and Coles 2003.
25. Amit and Zott 2001; Zott and Amit 2008.
26. 2003
27. *The Sun* 2012.
28. 2005.
29. Mascarenhas, Kesavan and Bernacchi 2004.
30. Arend 2006; Schindehutte, Morris and Kocak 2008.
31. Brown 1993, p. 28.

# References

Adam, S., Vocino, A. and Bednall, D. (2009). 'The World Wide Web in Modern Marketing's Contribution to Organisational Performance'. *Marketing Intelligence & Planning*, 27(1): 7–24.

Addis, M. and Podesta, S. (2005). 'Long Life to Marketing Research'. *European Journal of Marketing*, 39(3/4): 386–412.

Afuah, A. and Tucci, C. (2001). *Internet Business Models and Strategies.* (McGraw-Hill International, New York).

Aikena, K. D., Mackoyb, R., Shaw-Ching Liuc, B., Fetterb, R. and Osland, G. (2008). 'Dimensions of Internet Commerce Trust'. *Journal of Internet Commerce*, 6(4): 1–25.

Alleyne, R. (2005), 'Battle of Ikea: 20 hurt as Frenzied Mob Fights Over £49 Sofas on Opening Night'. Available at http://www.telegraph.co.uk/news/main.jhtml?xml=/news/2005/02/11/nikea11.xml. Accessed 7 October 2009.

Alreck, P. L. and Settle, R. B. (2007). 'Consumer Reactions to Online Behavioural Tracking and Targeting'. *Journal of Database Marketing & Customer Strategy Management.* 15: 11–23.

Alt, R. and Zimmermann, H. D. (2001). 'Introduction to Special Section-Business Models'. *Electronic Markets*, 11(1): 3–9.

Amit, R. and Zott, C. (2001). 'Value Creation in E-Business'. *Strategic Management Journal*, 22: 493–520.

Anitsal, I. and Schumann, D. W. (2007). 'Towards A Conceptualization of Customer Productivity'. *Journal of Marketing Theory and Practice.* Armonk: Fall 2007. 15(4): 349–65.

Arend, R. (2006). 'Bursting Bubbles: What the Internet Could Have Meant to Strategic Management Academia'. *Journal of Management Inquiry*, 15(4): 372–82.

Arndt, J. (1967). 'Role of Product-Related Conversations in the Diffusion of a New Product'. *Journal of Marketing Research*, 4(3): 291–5.

Arnold, S. (2002). 'Lessons Learned from the World's Best Retailers'. *International Journal of Retail & Distribution Management*, 30(11, 12): 562–70.

Autry, C., Hill, D. and O'Brien, M. (2007). 'Attitude toward the Customer: A Study of Product Returns Episodes'. *Journal of Managerial Issues*, 19: 315–40.

Avdeyeva, O. (2010). 'States Compliance with International Requirements: Gender Equality in EU Enlargement Countries'. *Political Research Quarterly*, 63/1, 203–17.

Baer, R. and Hill, D. (1994). 'Excuse Making: A Prevalent Company Response to Complaints?' *Journal of Consumer Satisfaction, Dissatisfaction and Complaining Behavior*, 7: 143–51.

Ballantyne, D. and Varey, R. J. (2008). 'The Service-Dominant Logic and the Future of Marketing'. *Journal of the Academy of Marketing Science*, 36, 11–14.

Balsamo, A. (2000). 'The Virtual Body in Cyberspace'. In D. Bell and B. M. Kennedy (eds) *The Cybercultures Reader*. (London and New York: Routledge).

Barrett, S. D. (2004). 'The Sustainability of the Ryanair Model'. *International Journal of Transport Management*, 2(2): 89–98.

Barrutia, J. M. and Echebarria, C. (2005). 'The Internet and Consumer Power: The Case of Spanish Retail Banking'. *Journal of Retailing and Consumer Services*, 12: 255–71.

Batt, R. and L. Moynihan (2002). 'The Viability of Alternative Call Centre Production Models'. *Human Resource Management Journal*, 12(4): 14–34.

BBC Watchdog (2008). http://www.bbc.co.uk/blogs/watchdog/2008/10/ryanairs_free_flights.html.

BBC (2010). 'Ryanair Payment Policy is "Puerile"', says OFT. 4 January 2010. Available at http://news.bbc.co.uk/1/hi/8438837.stm. Accessed 10 August 2011.

Beatty, S. and Smith, S. (1987). 'External Search Effort: An Investigation across Several Product Categories'. *Journal of Consumer Research*, 14: 83–95.

Bell, S., Menguc, B. and Stefani, S. (2004). 'When Customers Disappoint: A Model of Relational Internal Marketing and Customer Complaints'. *Journal of the Academy of Marketing Science*, 32(2): 112–26.

Bell, S. and Luddington, J. (2006). 'Coping with Customer Complaints'. *Journal of Service Research*, 8(3), 221–33.

Belobaba, P., Odoni, A. and Barnhart, C. (2009). *The Global Airline Industry*. (Chichester: Wiley & Sons).

Berry, L. (2000). 'Relationship Marketing of Services – Growing Interest, Emerging Perspectives'. In J. Sheth and A. Parvatiyar (eds) *Handbook of Relationship Marketing*. (London: Sage Publications), 149–70.

Berry, M. J. A. and Linoff, G. (2000). *Mastering Data Mining: The Art and Science of Customer Relationship Management*. (New York: Wiley).

Besanko, D., Dranove, D. and Shanley, M. (1996). *The Economics of Strategy*. (New York: John Wiley).

Binggeli, U. and Pompeo, L. (2007). 'The Battle for Europe's Low-Fare Flyers'. *The McKinsey Quarterly*. Available at http://www.mckinseyquarterly.com/PDFDownload.aspx. Accessed 23 January 2008.

Bolton, S. and Houlihan, M., (2005). 'The (Mis)Representation of Customer Service'. *Work, Employment & Society*, 19(4): 685–703.

Bonsu, S. K. and Darmody, A. (2008). 'Co-creating Second Life: Market_ Consumer Cooperation in Contemporary Economy'. *Journal of Macromarketing*, 28: 355–71.

Boru, B. (2006). 'Ryanair: The Cu Chulainn of Civil Avaiation'. *Journal of Strategic Marketing*, 14(1): 45–55.

Boshoff, C. (1997). 'An Experimental Study of Service Recovery Options'. *International Journal of Service Industry Management*, 8(2): 110–30.

Bowen, D. and Johnston R. (1999). 'Internal Service Recovery: Developing a New Construct'. *International Journal of Service Industry Management*, 2: 118–31.

Bowman, C. and Faulkner, D. (1996). *Competitve and Corporate Strategy*. (Irwin: London).

Box, T. and Texas, K. (2005). 'Ryanair (2005) Successful Low Cost Leadership'. *International Academy for Case Studies*, 13(3): 65–70.

Brady, M. and Cronin, J. (2001). 'Some New Thoughts on Conceptualizing Perceived Service Quality'. *Journal of Marketing*, 65: 34–49.

Brady, D. and Norris, W. (2009). 'Driving Conversion by Delivering More Value to the Customer in the Downturn'. Internet World, 29th April, London. Available at www.seminarstreams.com/app/content_play.asp?p id=268&mcid=130&sid=177. Accessed 3 June 2009.

Brennan, R., Baines, P. and Garneau, P. (2008). *Contemporary Strategic Marketing*. (Basingstoke: Palgrave Macmillan).

Briner, R. (2010). 'How Can I Help You Sir?' *People Management*, 2 November: 17–9.

Brookes, R. and Palmer, R. (2003), *The New Global Marketing Reality*. (Basingstoke: Palgrave Macmillan).

Brown, S. (1993). 'Postmodern Marketing'. *European Journal of Marketing*, 27(4): 19–34.

Brown, J. J. and Reingen, P. M. (1987). 'Social Ties and Word-Of-Mouth Referral Behaviour'. *The Journal of Consumer Research*, 14(3): 350–62.

Buhalis, D. (2004). 'eAirlines: Strategic and Tactical Use of ICTS in the Airline Industry'. *Information & Management*, 41(7): 805–25.

Burns, A. and Bush, R. (2003). *Marketing Research*. (New Jersey: Prentice Hall).

Button, K. (2003). 'Does the Theory of the "Core" Explain Why Airlines Fail to Cover Their Long-Run Costs of Capital?' *Journal of Air Transport Management*, 9: 5–14.

Button, K. and Nijkamp, P. (1997). 'Network Industries, Economic Stability and Spatial Integration'. Tinbergen Institute Discussion Papers 047/3.

Callaghan, G. and Thompson, P. (2001). 'Edwards Revisited: Technical Control and Call Centres'. *Economic and Industrial Democracy*, 22(1): 13–37.

Campanelli, M. (2006). 'FTC Studies Technology, Privacy Issues', *DM News*, 20th November.

Carrillat, F., Jaramillo, F. and Locander, W. (2004), 'Market-Driving Organizations: A Framework'. *Academy of Marketing Science Review*, 15: 1–14.

Charitou, C. and Markides, C. (2003). 'Responses to Disruptive Strategic Innovation'. *MIT Sloan Management Review*, 45: 55–63.

Chen, Q. and Chen, H-M. (2004). 'Exploring the Success Factors of eCRM Strategies in Practice'. *Database Marketing & Customer Strategy Management*, 11(4): 333–343.

Chesbrough, H. and Rosenbloom, R. (2002). 'The Role of the Business Model in Capturing Value from Innovation: Evidence from Xerox Corporation's Technology Spin-Off Companies'. *Industrial and Corporate Change*, 11(3): 529–55.

Chylinski, M. and Chu, A. (2010). 'Consumer Cynicism: Antecedents and Consequences'. *European Journal of Marketing*, 44(6), 796–837

Coad, T. (2006). 'The Future for 'Do-It-Yourself' Customer Service'. *Journal of Database Marketing & Customer Strategy Management*, 4: 324–30.

Colgate, M. and Danaher, P. (2000), 'Implementing a Customer Relationship Strategy: The Asymmetric Impact of Poor versus Excellent Execution'. *Journal of the Academy of Marketing Science*, 28(3): 375–87.

Collin-Jacques, C. (2004). 'Professionals at Work: A Study of Autonomy and Skill Utilization in Nurse Call Centres in England and Canada'. In S. Deery and N. Kinnie (eds), *Call Centres and Human Resource Management: A Cross-National Perspective*. (Basingstoke: Palgrave Macmillan).

Collinson, P. (2001). 'Scandal of Britain's Uncovered Drivers'. *Guardian* 24 March. Available at http://www.guardian.co.uk/Archive/Article/0,4273, 4158041,00.html. Accessed 17 July 2001.

Cooper, T. (2006). 'Enhancing Insight Discovery by Balancing the Focus of Analytics between Strategic and Tactical Levels'. *Database Marketing & Customer Strategy Management*, 13(4), 261–70.

Creaton, S. (2007). *Ryanair: The Full Story of the Controversial Low-cost Airline*. (London: Aurum Press).

Croft, J. (2004). 'Surge in Complaints over Banks by Public'. *Financial Times*, July 12. Available at http://search.ft.com/ftArticle?queryText= Surge+in+Complaints +over+Banks+by+Public&y=8&aje=true&x=15& id=060501007074. Accessed 23 June 2007.

D'Aveni, R. (1995). *Hypercompetitive Rivalries*. New York: Free Press.

D'Aveni, R. A., Dagnino, G. B. and Smith, K. G. (2010). 'The Age of Temporary Advantage'. *Strategic Management Journal*, 31(13): 1371–85.

Dabholkar, P. A. (1996). 'Consumer Evaluations of New Technology-Based Self-Service Options: An Investigation of Alternative Models of Service Quality'. *International Journal of Research in Marketing*, 13(1): 29–51.

Darling, J., Gabrielsson, M. and Seristo, H. (2007). 'Enhancing Contemporary Entrepreneurship'. *European Business Review*, 19: 4–11.

Datamonitor (2007). http://www.datamonitor.com/store/News/easyjet_ online_campaigns_fly_with_webtrends_analytics?productid=3B49BD68-7134-412F-843B-9C6D70BBE527.

Day, G. (2000), 'Managing Market Relationships', *Academy of Marketing Science Journal*, 28(1): 24–30.

Dean, A. and Terziovski, M. (2000), 'Quality Practices and Customer/Supplier Management in Australian Service Organizations: Untapped Potential', Working Paper Series, Monash University Department of Management, Melbourne.

Degeratu, A., Rangaswamy, A. and Wu, J. (2000). ,Consumer Choice Behavior in On-line and Traditional Supermarkets: The Effects of Brand Name, Price, and Other Search Attributes'. *InternationalJournal of Research in Marketing*, 17(1), pp. 55–78.

Dellande, S. and Nyer, P. (2007). 'Using Public Commitment to Gain Customer Compliance'. *Advances in Consumer Research*, 34: 249–55.

Dellande, S., Gilly, M. and Graham, J. (2004). 'Gaining Compliance and Losing Weight'. *Journal of Marketing*, 68: 78–91.

Deschamps, J. P. (2005), 'Different Leadership Skills for Different Innovation Strategies'. *Strategy & Leadership*, 33: 31–8.

Devi, B. and Aruna, N. (2006). 'Amazon's Foray into e-Grocery Market: Successful Venture?' ECCH Case Studies. Available at http://www.ecch.com/. Accessed on 7 October 2009.

Dick, A. S. and Basu, K. (1994). 'Customer Loyalty: Toward an Integrated Conceptual Framework'. *Journal of the Academy of Marketing Science*, 22(2): 99–113.

Doganis, R. (2006). *The Airline Business*, New York: Routledge.

Domanico, F. (2007). 'The European Airline Industry: Law and Economics'. *European Journal of Law Economics*, 23: 199–221.

Douglas, A. and Berendien, L. (2010). 'An Empirical Investigation into the Role of Personal-Related Factors on Corporate Travel Policy Compliance'. *Journal of Business Ethics*, 92(3): 451–61.

Dowling, G. R. and Staelin, R. (1994). 'A Model of Perceived Risk and Intended Risk-Handling Activity', *Journal of Consumer Research*, 21: 119–34.

Doyle, S. (2006), 'The Evolution of Self Service Environments and their Potential Business Impact'. *Database Marketing & Customer Strategy Management*, 13(3), 236–43.

Drucker, P. F. (1954). 'The Practice of Management'. (New York: Harper and Row).

Dubosson-Torbay, M., Osterwalder, A. and Pigneur, Y. (2002). 'E-Business Model Design, Classification and Measurements'. *Thunderbird International Business Review*, 44(1): 5–23.

Dyck, A. and Reinbergs, I. (1998). 'Comings to Grips with Deregulation: Bay State Gas'. ECCH Case Studies. Available at http://www.ecch.com/. Accessed 7 October 2009.

Epsilon (2007). 'EasyJet: Email Marketing Flies High with Epsilon International'. Available at http://72.30.186.56/search/cache?ei=UTF-8&p=easyJet+DREAMmail+2005&rd=r1&fr=yfp-t-501&u=www.

epsilon.com/international/pdfs/Epsilon_International_easyJet_case_study.pdf&w=easyjet+%22easy+jet%22+dreammail+2005&d=CE6qn0fi SCVd&icp=1&.intl=uk. Accessed 17 January 2008.

Fawcett, S. E. and Farris, M. T. (1998). 'Contestable Markets and Airline Adaptability Under Deregulation'. *Transportation Journal*, 29: 12–24.

Fayyad, U. (2001). 'The Digital Physics of Data Mining'. *Communications of the ACM*, 44(3): 62–5.

Felton, A. (1959). 'Making the Marketing Concept Work'. *Harvard Business Review*, 37, (July/Aug): 55–65.

Fernie, S. and Metcalf, D. (1998). *(Not) Hanging on the Telephone: Payment Systems in the New Sweatshops*. (London: Centre for Economic Performance, London School of Economics and Political Science).

Fiore, F. (2001). *E-Marketing Strategies*. (Indianapolis, In.: QUE).

Fletcher, R. (2007). 'Ikea is Abusing Our Loyalty'. Available at http://blogs. telegraph.co.uk/business/talesofthehighstreet/aug07/ikea-standards. htm. Accessed 7 October 2009.

Ford, D. (1990). *Understanding Business Markets*. (London: Academic Press).

Frow, P. and Payne, A. (2007). 'Towards the "Perfect" Customer Experience'. *Journal of Brand Management*, 15: 89–101.

Gilmore, A. (2001), 'Call Centre Management: Is Service Quality a Priority?'. *Managing Service Quality*, 1(3), pp. 153–9.

Glass, J., McKillop, D. and Rasaratnam, S. (2010). 'Irish Credit Unions: Investigating Performance Determinants and the Opportunity Cost of Regulatory Compliance'. *Journal of Banking & Finance*, 34(1): 67–77.

Godes, D. and Mayzlin, D. (2004). 'Using Online Conversations to Study Word-of-Mouth Communication'. *Marketing Science*, 23(4): 545–60.

Goodman, J. (1992). 'Leveraging the Customer Database to Your Competitive Advantage'. *Direct Marketing*, 55(8): 26–7.

Goss, J. (1995). 'We Know Who You are and We Know Where You live: The Instrumental Rationality of Geodemographic Systems'. *Economic Geography*, 71(2): 171–98.

Greenley, G., Hooley, G., Broderick, A. and Rudd, J. (2004). 'Strategic Planning Differences among Different Multiple Stakeholder Orientation Profiles'. *Journal of Strategic Marketing*, 12(3) 163–82.

Grol, P. and Schoch, C. (1998). 'IKEA: Culture as Competitive Advantage' ECCH Case Studies. Available at http://www.ecch.com/. Accessed 8 October 2009.

Grönroos, C. (1990). *Service Management and Marketing: Managing the Moments of Truth in Service Competition*. (New York: Lexington Books).

Grönroos, C. (1995) 'Relationship Marketing: The Strategy Continuum'. *Journal of the Academy of Marketing Science*, 23(4): 252–4.

Gruen, T., Summers, J. and Acito, F. (2000). 'Relationship Marketing Activities, Commitment, and Membership Behavior Activities'. *Journal of Marketing* 64(3): 1–17.

Gummesson, E. (1999). *Total Relationship Marketing: Rethinking Marketing Management from 4ps to 30Rs.* (Oxford: Butterworth-Heinemann).

Haig, M. (2004). *The e-Marketing handbook.* (UK: Kogan Page).

Hair, J. F. J., Money, A. H., Samouel, P. and Page, M. (2007). *Research Methods for Business.* (Chichester: John Wiley & Sons Ltd).

Harari, O. (1997). 'Thank Heavens for Complainers'. *Management Review*, 86: 25–9.

Harrison, T., Waite, K. and Hunter, G. L. (2006). 'The Internet, Information and Empowerment'. *European Journal of Marketing*, 40(9/10):. 972–93.

Hausman, A. and Johnston, W. (2010). 'The Impact of Coercive and Non-Coercive Forms of Influence on Trust, Commitment, and Compliance in Supply Chains'. *Industrial Marketing Management*, 39: 519–26.

Helm, A. (2004). 'Cynics and Skeptics: Consumer Dispositional Trust'. *Advances in Consumer Research*, 31: 245–51.

Henderson, Iain and Murray, D. (2005). 'Prioritising and Deploying Data Quality Improvement Activity'. *Database Marketing & Customer Strategy Management*, 12(2): 113–19.

Henkel, S., Tomczak, T., Heitmann, M. and Herrmann, A. (2007). 'Managing Brand Consistent Employee Behaviour: Relevance and Managerial Control Of Behavioural Branding'. *Journal of Product and Brand Management*, 16(5): 310–20.

Hennig-Thurau, T., Gwinner, K. P., Walsh, G. and Gremler, D. D. (2004). 'Electronic Word-of-Mouth via Consumer-Opinion Platforms: What Motivates Consumers to Articulate Themselves on the Internet?' *Journal of Interactive Marketing*, 18(1): 38–52

Heskett, T., Jones, O., Loveman, G., Earl Sasser Jr., W. and Schlesinger, L. (2008). 'Putting the Service Profit Chain to Work'. *Harvard Business Review.* Available at http://www.hbsp.harvard.edu/hbsp/hbo/articles/article.jsp?articleID=4460&ml_action=get-article&pageNumber=1&ml. Accessed 3 August 2009.

Hibbs, D. and Piculescu, V. (2010). 'Tax Toleration and Tax Compliance: How Government Affects the Propensity of Firms to Enter the Unofficial Economy'. *American Journal of Political Science*, 54(1): 18–34.

Hitt, M., Keats, B. and DeMarie, S. (1998). 'Navigating in the New Competitive Landscape: Building Strategic Flexibility and Competitive Advantage in the 21st Century'. *Academy of Management Executive*, 12(4): 22–42.

Hodgson, D. (2002). '"Know Your Customer": Marketing, Governmentality and the "New Consumer" of Fnancial Services'. *Management Decision*, 40(4): 318–28.

Horkheimer, M. and Adorno, T. W. (1944). 'The Culture Industry: Enlightenment as Mass Deception'. In *Dialectic of Enlightenment* (J. Cumming, Trans.). (New York: Continuum), 123–5.

Humphrey, R. and Ashforth, B. (1994). 'Cognitive Scripts and Prototypes in Service Encounters'. In T. Swartz, D. Bowen and S. Brown (eds) *Advances in Service Marketing and Management.* (Greenwich, Ct.: JAI Press), 175–99.

Humphreys, A. (2006). 'The Consumer as Foucauldian "Object of Knowledge"'. *Social Science Computer Review*, 24: 296.

Hunger, D. and Wheelen, T. (2007). *Essentials of strategic management.* (Upper Saddle River, New Jersey: Prentice Hall).

Huppertz, J. (2003). 'An Effort Model of First-Stage Complaining Behaviour'. *Journal of Consumer Satisfaction, Dissatisfaction and Complaining Behavior,*16: 132–44.

Ilinitch, A.Y, D'Aveni, R. A and Lewin A. Y. (1996). 'New Organizational Forms and Strategies for Managing in Hyper-Competitive Environments'. *Organization Science*, 7(3): 211–20.

Inderst, R. (2010). 'Misselling (Financial) Products: The Limits for Internal Compliance'. *Economics Letters*, 106(1): 35–8.

Irish Times (2010). 'Ryanair ner bottom of "ethical ranking" list. 02 Feb 2010'. Avaialble at http://www.irishtimes.com/newspaper/ireland/2010/0201/1224263502392.html. Accessed on 3 April 2011.

Jackson, T. W. (2007). 'Personalisation and CRM'. *Database Marketing & Customer Strategy Management*, 15(1), 24–36.

Jarvenpaa, S. L., Tractinsky, N. and Vitale, M. (2000). 'Consumer Trust in an Internet Store'. *Information Technology and Management,* 1(1, 2): 45–71

Jaworski, B. and Kohli, A. (1993). 'Market Orientation'. *Journal of Marketing*, 57: 53–81.

Jenkinson, A. (2006). 'Do Organisations Now Understand the Importance of Information in Providing Excellent Customer Experience?' *Database Marketing & Customer Strategy Management*, 13(4): 248–60.

Johnson, R. (2006). 'Strategy, Success, a Dynamic Economy and the 21st Century Manager'. *The Business Review*, 5: 23–9.

Johnson, D. and Grayson, K. (2005). 'Cognitive and Affective Trust in Service Relationships'. *Journal of Business Research*, 58(4): 500–7.

Johnston, R. and Clark, G. (2005). *Service Operations Management: Improving Service Delivery.* 2nd edn. (Harlow: Financial Times Prentice Hall).

Judge, T., Erez, A., Thoresen, C. and Bono, J. (2002). 'Are Measures of Self-Esteem, Neuroticism, Locus of Control, and Generalized Self-Efficacy Indicators of a Common Core Construct?' *Journal of Personality and Social Psychology*; 83: 693–701.

Kadet, A. (2006). 'Buyer Beware'. *SmartMoney*, May: 90–5.

Kanousi, A. (2005). 'An Empirical Investigation of the Role of Culture on Service Recovery Expectations'. *Managing Service Quality*, 1: 57–69.

Kasabov, E. (2004). 'Power and Disciplining: Bringing Foucault to Marketing'. *Irish Marketing Review* 17(1): 3–12.

Kasabov, E. (2007). 'Power and Opposition to Power: Mirror Realities of Complex Consumption Interactions'. *Journal of Marketing Theory and Practice*, 15(4): 365–75.

Kasabov, E. and Warlow, A. (2009). 'Automated Marketing and E-Marketing Practices of "Customer Compliance" Providers'. *Journal of Direct, Data and Digital Marketing Practice*, 11(1): 30–50.

Kasabov, E. (2010). 'The Compliant Customer'. *MIT Sloan Management Review*, 51(3): 18–9.

Kasouf, C., Celuch, K. and Strieter, J. (1995). 'Consumer Complaints as Market Intelligence: Orienting Context and Conceptual Framework'. *Journal of Consumer Satisfaction, Dissatisfaction and Complaining Behavior*, 8: 59–68.

Keen, C., M. Wetzels, K. de Ruyter and R. Feinberg (2004). 'E-tailers versus Retailers: Which Factors Determine Consumer Preferences'. *Journal of Business Research*, 57(7): 685–95.

Kelley, S., Hoffman, K. and Davis, M. (1993). 'A Typology of Retail Failures and Recoveries'. *Journal of Retailing*, 69(4): 429–63.

Kim, E., Nam, D. and Stimpert, J. (2004). 'Testing the Applicability of Porter's Generic Strategies in the Digital Age: A Study of Korean Cyber Malls'. *Journal of Business Strategies*, 21: 19–45.

King, R. (2008). 'Building a Brand with Widgets'. *BusinessWeek* 3 March. Available at http://www.businessweek.com/technology/content/feb2008/tc20080303_000743.htm. Accessed 17 March 2008.

Ko, K., Mendeloff, J. and Gray, W. (2010). 'The Role of Inspection Sequence in Compliance with the US Occupational Safety and Health Adminsitration's (OSHA) Standards'. *Regulation & Governance*, 4(1): 48–70.

Kohli, A. and Jaworski, B. (1990). 'Market Orientation: The Construct, Research Propositions, and Managerial Implications'. *Journal of Marketing*, 54, (April): 1–18.

Kotler, P. (2000). *Marketing Management*. (Upper Saddle River, NJ: Prentice Hall).

Kotler, P. and Keller, K. (2006). *Marketing management*. (New Delhi: Prentice Hall).

Kozinets, R. V. (2002). 'Can Consumers Escape The Market? Emancipatory Illuminations from Burning Man'. *Journal of Consumer Research*, 29(1): 20–38.

Labe Jr., R. P. (1994). 'Database Marketing Increases Prospecting Effectiveness at Merrill Lynch'. *Interfaces*, 24(5), 1–12.

Lawler, E. and Worley, C. (2006). *Built to Change: How to Achieve Sustained Organizational Effectiveness*. (Jossey-Bass, San Francisco, Ca.).

Lengnick-Hall, C. and Wolff, J. (1999). 'Similarities and Contradictions in the Core Logic of Three Strategy Research Streams'. *Strategic Management Journal*, 20(12): 1109–32.

Lester, T. (2006). 'The Cost of Not Caring for Your Customers'. *FT.com*. Published January 19.

Liljander, V. and Roos, I. (2002). 'Customer-Relationship Levels – from Spurious to True Relationships'. *Journal of Services Marketing*, 16(7): 593–614.

Lindgreen, A., Palmer, R. and Vanhamme, J. (2004). 'Contemporary Marketing Practice: Theoretical Propositions and Practical Implications'. *Journal of Marketing Intelligence*. 22(6): 673–92.

Lusch, R. F. and Vargo, S. L. (2006). *The Service-Dominant Logic of Marketing: Dialog, Debate, and Directions*. (Armonk, NY: M. E. Sharpe).

Macdonald, C. L. and Sirianni, C. (1996). 'The Service Society and the Changing Experience of Work'. In C. L. Macdonald and C. Sirianni (eds), *Working in the Service Society*. (Philadelphia, PA: Temple University Press), 1–26.

Magretta, J. (2002). 'Why Business Models Matter'. *Harvard Business Review*, 80: 86–93 (May).

Mahadevan, B. (2000). 'Business Models for Internet Based E-Commerce: an Anatomy'. *California Management Review*, 42: 55–69.

Malone, T., Yates, J. and Benjamin, R. (1987). 'Electronic Markets and Electronic Hierarchies'. *Communications of the ACM*, 30(6): 484–97.

Mascarenhas, O., Kesavan, R. and Bernacchi, M. (2004), 'Customer Value-Chain Involvement for Co-Creating Customer Delight', *Journal of Consumer Marketing*, 21(7), 486.

Masters, A. (2010). 'A Theory of Minimum Wage Compliance (or Voluntary Recognition of Unions)'. *Labour Economics*, 17(1), 215–23.

Mattson, L. (1997). '"Relationship Marketing" and the "markets as Networks Approach"'. *Journal of Marketing Management*, 13(5): 447–61.

Maxham, J. G., (2001). 'Service Recovery's Influence on Consumer Satisfaction, Positive Word-of-Mouth, and Purchase Intentions'. *Journal of Business Research*, 54(1): 11–24.

McCollough, M., Berry, L. and Yadav, M., (2000). 'An Empirical Investigation of Customer Satisfaction after Service Failure and Recovery'. *Journal of Service Research*, 3(2): 121–37.

McCosker, P. (2003). 'EasyJet: The Spectacular Growth of Low Cost Airlines'. ECCH Case Studies. Available at http://www.ecch.com/. Accessed 7 October 2009.

McKitterick, J. B. (1957). 'What is the Marketing Management Concept'. In F. M. Bass (ed.), *The Frontiers in Marketing Thought*. (Chicago: American Marketing Association), 71–82.

McNamara, C. (1972). 'The Present Status of the Marketing Concept'. *Journal of Marketing*, 36, (Jan): 50–7.

McWilliam, G. (2000). 'Building Stronger Brands through Online Communities'. *Sloan Management Review*, Spring: 43–54.

Mehta, K. (2008), 'E-Commerce: On-Line Retail Distribution Strategies and Global Challenges'. *The Business Review*, 9(2): pp. 31–6.

Mehta, R. and Sivadas, E. (1995). 'Comparing Response Rates and Response Content in Mail versus Electronic Mail Surveys'. *Journal of the Market Research Society*, 37: 429–39.

Meuter, M., Ostrom, A., Rountree, R. and Bitner, M. J. (2000). 'Self-Service Technologies: Understanding Customer Satisfaction with Technology-Based Service Encounters'. *Journal of Marketing*, 64(3): 50–64.

Meyer, A. (1982). 'Adapting to Environmental Jolts'. *Administrative Science Quarterly*, 27(4): 515–37.

Mitchell, V-W. (1999). 'Consumer Perceived Risk: Conceptualisations and Models'. *European Journal of Marketing*, 33(1/2): 163–95.

Mitchell, D. and Coles, C. (2003). 'Building Better Business Models'. *Leader to Leader,* 17(summer): 12–17.

Mitussis, D., O'Malley, L. and Patterson, M. (2006). 'Mapping the Re-Engagement of CRM with Relationship Marketing'. *European Journal of Marketing*, 40(5/6): 572–89.

Morris, J. A. and Feldman, D. C. (1997). 'Managing Emotions in the Workplace'. *Journal of Managerial Issues*, 9: 257–74.

Morris, M., Schindehutte, M. and Allen, J. (2005). 'The Entrepreneur's Business Model: Toward a Unified Perspective'. *Journal of Business Research*, 58: 726–35.

Murphy, T. (2000). *Web Rules: How the Internet is Changing the Way Consumers Make Choices.* (Chicago: Dearborn).

Narver, J. and Slater, S. (1990) 'The Effect of A Market Orientation on Business Profitability'. *Journal of Marketing*, 54(4): 20–35.

Naylor, G. (2003). 'The Complaining Customer: A Service Provider's Best Friend?' *Journal of Consumer Satisfaction, Dissatisfaction and Complaining Behavior*, 16: 241–8.

Newing, R. (2007). 'Role of Managers: Leaders Must Set the Best Example'. *Financial Times*, 12 November. Available at http://search.ft.com/ftArti cle?queryText=dissatisfied+customer+&page=2&aje=false&id=0711120 00312&ct=0. Accessed 7 October 2009.

Nijsen, A., Hudson, J., Müller, C., van Paridon, K. and Thurik, R. (eds) (2009). *Business Regulation and Public Policy: The Costs and Benefits of Compliance.* (New York: Springer).

Nonaka, I. (1994). 'A Dynamic Theory of Organizational Knowledge Creation'. *Organization Science*, 5: 14–38.

Oliver, R. L. (1997). *Satisfaction: A Behavioral Perspective on the Consumer.* (Boston: McGraw Hill).

Olsen, L. and Johnson, M. (2003). 'Service Equity, Satisfaction, and Loyalty: From Transaction-Specific to Cumulative Evaluation'. *Journal of Service Research*, 5(3): 184–95.

Osarenkhoe, A. (2008). 'What Characterises the Culture of a Market-Oriented Organisation Applying a Customer-Intimacy Philosophy?' *Journal of Database Marketing & Customer Strategy Management*, 15(3): 169–90.

Palmer, A., Beggs, R. and McMullan C. K. (2000). 'Equity and Repurchase Intention Following Service Failure'. *Journal of Services Marketing*, 14(6): 513–28.

Palmer, A. (2004). *Principles of Services Marketing.* (Maidenhead: McGraw-Hill).

Parasuraman, A., Zeithaml, V.A. and Berry, L.L. (1985). 'A Conceptual Model of Service Quality and Its Implications for Future Research'. *Journal of Marketing*, 49: 41–50.

Parasuraman, A., Zeithaml, V.A. and Berry, L.L. (1988). 'SERVQUAL: A Multiple-Item Scale for Measuring Consumer Perceptions of Service Quality'. *Journal of Retailing*, 64(1): 12–40.

Pavlou, P. (2003), 'Consumer Acceptance of Electronic Commerce: Integrating Trust and Risk with the Technology Acceptance Model'. *International Journal of Electronic Commerce*, 7(3): 101–34.

Payne, A. F., Store Acka, K. and Frow, P. (2008). 'Managing the Co-Creation of Value'. *Journal of the Academy of Marketing Science*, 36: 83–96.

Pires, G. D., Stanton, J. and Rita, P. (2006). 'The Internet, Consumer Empowerment and Marketing Strategies', *European Journal of Marketing*, 40(9): 936–49.

Pitta, D. and Fowler, D. (2005). 'Internet Community Forums: An Untapped Resource for Consumer Marketers'. *Journal of Consumer Marketing*. 5: 265–74.

Porter, M. (1980) *Competitive Strategy: Techniques for Analyzing Industries and Competitors*. (New York: Free Press).

Porter, M. E. (1985). *Competitive Advantage: Creating and Sustaining Superior Performance*. (New York: Free Press).

Prahalad, C. K. and Ramaswamy, V. (2000). 'Co-opting Customer Competence'. *Harvard Business Review*, 78: 79–87.

Prahalad, C. K. and Ramaswamy, V. (2004). *The Future of Competition : Co-Creating Unique Value with Customers,* (Boston (Mass.), Harvard Business School Press).

Proff, H. (2000), 'Hybrid Strategies as A Strategic Challenge – the Case of the German Automotive Industry'. *Omega*, 28: 541–53.

Puga Leal, R. and Pereira, Z. (2003). 'Service Recovery at A Financial Institution'. *International Journal of Quality & Reliability Management*, 20: 646–63.

Quader, M. (2007). 'The Strategic Implications of Electronic Commerce for Small and Medium Sized Enterprises'. *Journal of Services Research*, 7(1): 25–60.

Radhika, A. (2003). *Meg Whitman: The Driving Force behind eBay.* ECCH Case Studies. Available at http://www.ecch.com/. Accessed 7 October 2009.

Reid, A. and Catterall, M. (2005). 'Invisible Data Quality Issues in a CRM Implementation'. *Database Marketing & Customer Strategy Management*, 12(4): 305–14.

Reisch, L. A. (2001). /The Internet and Sustainable Consumption: Perspectives on a Janus Face'. *Journal of Consumer Policy*, 24: 251–86.

Rezabakhsh, B., Bornemann, D., Hansen, U. and Schrader, U. (2006). 'Consumer Power: A Comparison of the Old Economy and the Internet Economy'. *Journal of Consumer Policy*, 29: 3–36.

Rha, J.-Y. and Widdows, R. (2002). 'The Internet and the Consumer: Countervailing Power Revisited'. *Prometheus*, 20: 107–18.

Riegelsberger, J., Sasse, M.A. and McCarthy, J. D. (2003). 'The Researcher's Dilemma: Evaluating Trust in Computer-Mediated Communication'. *International Journal of Human-Computer Studies*, 58: 759–81.

Robinson, J. (2000). 'Deregulation and Regulatory Backlash in Health Care'. *California Management Review*, 43(1): 13–33.

Rud, O. (2001). *Data Mining Cookbook: Modeling Data for Marketing, Risk and Customer Relationship Management*. New York: Wiley.

Rumelt, R. P., Schendel, D. and Teece, D. J. (1994). *Fundamental Issues in Strategy: A Research Agenda*. Boston, MA: Harvard Business School Press.

Rungtusanatham, M., Salvador, F., Forza, C. and Choi, T., (2003). 'Supply-Chain Linkages and Operational Performance: A Resource-Based-View Perspective'. *International Journal of Operations & Production Management*, 23: 1084–99.

Russell, B. (2007). '"You Gotta Lie to it": Software Applications and the Management of Technological Change in a Call Centre'. *New Technology, Work and Employment*, 22: 132–45.

Rust, R. and Chung, T. (2006). 'Marketing Models of Service and Relationships'. *Marketing Science*, 25(6): 560–83.

Sam, A. (2010). 'Impact of Government-Sponsored Pollution Prevention Practices on Environmental Compliance and Enforcement'. *Journal of Regulatory Economics*, 37/3: 266–86.

Schindehutte, M., Morris, M. and Kocak, A. (2008). 'Understanding Market-Driving Behavior: The Role of Entrepreneurship'. *Journal of Small Business Management*, 46/1: 4–26.

Schoenbachler, D., Gordon, G., Foley, D. and Spellman, L. (1997). 'Understanding Consumer Database Marketing'. *Journal of Consumer Marketing*, 1: 5–19.

Schroeder, J. and Salzer-Morling, M. (2006). *Brand Culture*. (Routledge: Abingdon).

Schroter, H. G. (1997). 'Marketing als angewandte Sozialtechnik und Veranderungen im Konsumverhalten'. In H. Siegrist, H. Kaelble and J. Kocka (eds) *Europaische Konsumgeschichte*. (Frankfurt: Campus), 615–47.

Scott, D. (2008). 'A Case Study in Applied Social Marketing: Developing an Occupational Satefy and Health Product'. *Social Marketing Quarterly*, 14/4: 89–98.

Sebastiao, H. and Golicic, S. (2008). 'The Utilization of E-Commerce by Traditional Supply Chain Strategy for Nascent Firms in Emerging Technology Markets'. *Journal of Business Logistics*, 29(1): 75–92.

Senior, B. and Fleming, J. (2006). *Organizational Change*. (Essex: FT Prentice Hall).

Seyfang, G. (2007). 'Growing Sustainable Consumption Communities: The Case of Local Organic Food Networks'. *International Journal of Sociology and Social Policy*, 27(3/4): 120–34.

Shankar, A., Cherrier, H. and Canniford, R. (2006). 'Consumer Empowerment: A Foucauldian Interpretation'. *European Journal of Marketing*, 40(9): 1013–30.

Shaw, D. (2007). 'Consumer Voters in Imagined Communities'. *International Journal of Sociology and Social Policy*, 3: 135–51.

Shin, J. and Park, Y. (2009). 'On the Creation and Evaluation of E-Business Model Variants: The Case of Auction'. *Industrial Marketing Management*, 38: 324–37.

Shipman, A. (2001). 'Privatized Production, Socialized Consumption? Old Producer Power behind the New Consumer Sovereignty'. *Review of Social Economy*, 59, 331–52.

Shipman, A. (2007, October 12). 'Trading Rules and Accountings Check Foil Buyer Bribery at IKEA'. Available at Finance Week: www.financeweek. co.uk/cgibin/item.cgi?id=5612&d=11&h=24&f=254. Accessed 25 February 2008.

Silverman, G. (1997). 'How to Harness the Awesome Power of Word of Mouth'. *Direct Marketing*, 60(7): 32–7.

Singh, J. and Wilkes, R. (1996). 'When Consumers Complain: A Path Analysis of the Key Antecedents of Consumer Complaint Response Estimates'. *Journal of the Academy of Marketing Science*, 24: 350–65.

Singh, R. and Singh, L. (2008). 'Blogs: Emerging Knowledge Management Tools for Entrepreneurs to Enhance Marketing Efforts'. *Journal of Internet Commerce*, 7(4): 470–84.

Sirmon, D. G., Hitt, M. A., Arregle, J. and Campbell, J. T. (2010). 'The Dynamic Interplay of Capability Strengths and Weaknesses: Investigating the Bases of Temporary Competitive Advantage'. *Strategic Management Journal*, 31: 1386–409.

Skalen, P., Fellesson, M. and Fougere, M. (2006). 'The Governmentality of Marketing Discourse', *Scandinavian Journal of Management*, 22: 275–91.

Smart, D. and Martin, C. (1992). 'Manufacturer Responsiveness to Consumer Correspondence: An Empirical Investigation of Consumer Perceptions'. *Journal of Consumer Affairs*, 26: 104–28.

Smith, C. (2006). 'Bigger, Bluer, Cheaper, Better'. *Marketing*, Jan 25, p. 27.

Smith, B., Gunther, D. P., Venkateshwara, B. R. and Ratliff R. M. (2001). 'E-Commerce and Operations Research in Airline Planning, Marketing, and Distribution'. *Interfaces*, Mar/Apr, 31(2): 38–55.

Sotto, R. (1997). 'The Virtual Organization'. *Accounting, Management and Information Technology*, 7(1): 37–51.

Spencer-Matthews, S. and Lawley, M. (2006). 'Improving Customer Service: Issues in Customer Contact Management'. *European Journal of Marketing*, 40(1/2): 218–32.

Stalk, G. and Lachenauer, R. (2004). 'Hardball: Five Killer Strategies for Trouncing the Competition'. *Harvard Business Review*, 82(4): 62–71.

Stegman, M. (2008). 'Business Consultant Compliance – Reminders from the OIG's Special Advisory Bulletin'. *Journal of Health Care Compliance*, 10/6: 55–61.

Steinauer, J. (1997). 'The Face of the Sale'. *Incentives*, 171: 48–50.

Stewart, D. W., Pavlou, P. A. and Ward, S. (2002). 'Media Influences on Marketing Communications'. In J. Bryant and D. Zillmann (eds) *Media Effects: Advances in Theory and Research*. (Hillsdale, NJ: Erlbaum), pp. 353–96.

Stockdale, R. (2007), 'Managing Customer Relationships in the Self-service Environment of E-tourism', *Journal of Vacation Marketing*, 13(3), 205–19.

Strauss, J. and Frost, R. (2001). *E-Marketing*. (Upper Saddle River, NJ: Prentice Hall).

Stremersch, S. and Van Dyck, W. (2009). 'Marketing of the Life Sciences: A New Framework and Research Agenda for a Nascent Field'. *Journal of Marketing*, 73(July): 4–30.

Sun, The (2012). Source: http://www.thesun.co.uk/sol/homepage/news/4097747/Ryan-mighty.html.

Sureshchandar, G. C., Rajendran, C. and Anantharaman, R. N. (2002). 'The Relationship between Service Quality and Customer Satisfaction – a Factor-Specific Approach'. *Journal of Service Marketing,* 16(4): 363–79.

Szymanski, D. M. and Hise, R. T. (2000). 'E-Satisfaction: An Initial Examination'. *Journal of Retailing*, 76: 309–22.

Szymanski, D. M. and Henard, D. H. (2001). 'Customer Satisfaction: A Meta-Analysis of the Empirical Evidence', *Journal of the Academy of Marketing Science*, 29: 16–35.

Tapp, A. and Hughes, T. (2004). 'New Technology and the Changing Role of Marketing'. *Marketing Intelligence & Planning*, 22(3): 284–96.

Taylor, P. and Bain, P. (1999). '"An Assembly Line in the Head": Work and Employee Relations in the Call Centre'. *Industrial Relations Journal*, 30: 101–17.

Taylor, W. (2009). 'Why Ryanair's Bathroom Plan Sort of Makes Sense'. Available at http://blogs.hbr.org/taylor/2009/02/low_costs_high_dudgeon_are_you.html. Accessed 7 October 2010.

Thiétart, R. A. and Forgues, B. (1995). 'Chaos Theory and Organization'. *Organization Science*, 6: 19–31.

Thomas, L. and D'Aveni R. (2009). 'The Changing Nature of Competition in the U.S. Manufacturing Sector, 1950 to 2002'. *Strategic Organization*, 7(4): 387–431.

Tomlinson, A. (2002). 'Being Nice Takes its Toll'. *Canadian HR Reporter,* 15: 1–13.

Tomlinson, H. and Evans, R. (2005). 'Tesco Stocks Up on Inside Knowledge of Shoppers' Lives'. *Guardian* 20 September. Available at http://www.guardian.co.uk/business/2005/sep/20/freedomofinformation.supermarkets. Accessed 15 February 2006.

Tudhope, L., Prinsloo, M. and Pitt, L. (2007). 'Physician Compliance and Market Demographics'. *Journal of Medical Marketing*, 7/1: 64–71.

Turban, E, Lee, J., King, D., and Chung, H. M. (2002). *Electronic Commerce: A Managerial Perspective*, 2nd edn. (Upper Saddle River, NJ: Prentice Hall).

Turban, E., Rainer, R.K. and Potter, R. E.(2001). *Introduction to Information Technology*. (John Wiley & Sons, New York).

Turow, J. Feldman, L. and Meltzer, K. (2005). 'Open to Exploitation: American Shoppers Online and Offline'. University of Pennsylvania's Annenberg School for Communication, Philadelphia.

Urban, G. L. (2003). 'The Trust Imperative'. Cambridge, MA: Massachusetts Institute of Technology, Sloan School of Management. Working Paper 4302–03.

Van Dijke, M. and Verboon, P. (2010). 'Trust in Authorities as A Boundary Condition to Procedural Fairness Effects on Tax Compliance'. *Journal of Economic Psychology*, 31/1: 80–91

Varadarajan, R. and Yadav, M. (2002). 'Marketing Strategy and the Internet: An Organizing Framework'. *Journal of the Academy of Marketing Science* 30/4: 296–312.

Vargo, S. L. and Lusch, R. F. (2004). 'Evolving to a New Dominant Logic for Marketing'. *The Journal of Marketing*, 68(1) (Jan.): 1–17.

Vriens, M. and Grigsby, M. (2001). 'Building Profitable Online Customer–Brand Relationships'. *Marketing Management*, 10(4): 34–9.

Warrier, D. (2007). 'Evolution of eBay: Meg Whitman's Success Strategies'. ECCH Case Studies. Available at http://www.ecch.com/. Accessed 7 October 2009.

Weill, P. and Vitale, M. (2001). *Place to Space: Migrating to E-business Models*. (Harvard Business School Press, Boston, MA).

Weun, S., Beatty, S.E. and Jones, M.A. (2004). 'The Impact of Service Failure Severity on Service Recovery Evaluations and Post-Recovery Relationships'. *Journal of Services Marketing*, 18(2): 133–46.

Wheelen, T. and Hunger, D. (2002). *Strategic management and business policy*. (Upper Saddle River, NJ: Prentice-Hall).

Wiggins, R. R. and Ruefli, T. W. (2002). 'Sustained Competitive Advantage: Temporal Dynamics and the Incidence and Persistence of Superior Economic Performance'. *Organizational Science*, January-February, 13(1): 81–105.

Wiggins, R. and Ruefli, T. (2005). 'Schumpeter's Ghost: Is Hypercompetition Making the Best of Times Shorter?' *Strategic Management Journal*, 26(10): 887–911.

Wilk, E. and Fensterseifer, J. E. (2003). 'Use of Resource-Based View in Industrial Cluster Strategic Analysis'. *International Journal of Operations & Production Management*, 23(9): 995–1009.

Wirtz, B. and Lihotzky, N. (2003). 'Customer Retention Management in the B2C Electronic Business'. *Long Range Planning*, 36: 517–32.

Wirtz, J. and Mattila, A. (2004). 'Consumer Responses to Compensation, Speed of Recovery and Apology after a Service Failure'. *International Journal of Service Industry Management*, 15(2): 150–66.

Wyner, G. (2008). 'Marketing Evolution'. *Marketing Management*, 17(2): 8–9.

Zaid, A. (1995). 'Measuring and Monitoring Service Quality at Malaysia Airlines'. *Managing Service Quality*, 2: 25–7.

Zakon, R. (2005), 'Hobbes' Internet Timeline 1993–2005', the list of references illustrated available at www.zakon.org/robert/internet/timeline/. Accessed 9 November 2008.

Zeithaml, V., Parasuraman, A. and Berry, L. L. (1985). 'Problem and Strategies in Services Marketing'. *Journal of Marketing*, 49(1): 33–46.

Zott, C., Amit, R. and Donlevy, J. (2000). 'Strategies for Value Creation in E-commerce: Best Practice in Europe'. *European Management Journal*, 18(5): 463–75.

Zott, C. and Amit, R. (2007). 'Business Model Design and the Performance of Entrepreneurial Firms;. *OrganizationScience*, 18(2): 181–99.

Zott, C. and Amit, R. (2008). 'The Fit between Product Market Strategy and Business Model: Implications for Firm Performance'. *Strategic Management Journal*, 29: 1–26.

Zwick, D. and Dholakia, N. (2004a). 'Consumer Subjectivity in the Age of Internet'. *Information and Organization*, 14: 211–36.

Zwick, D. and Dholakia, N. (2004b).'Whose Identity is it Anyway'? *Journal of Macromarketing*, 24: 31–43.

Zwick, D., Bonsu, S. K. and Darmody, A. (2008). 'Putting Consumers to Work: "Co-creation" and New Marketing Govern-Mentality'. *Journal of Consumer Culture* 8(2): 163–96.

# Index

GPSR Compliance
The European Union's (EU) General Product Safety Regulation (GPSR) is a set
of rules that requires consumer products to be safe and our obligations to
ensure this.

If you have any concerns about our products, you can contact us on

ProductSafety@springernature.com

In case Publisher is established outside the EU, the EU authorized
representative is:

Springer Nature Customer Service Center GmbH
Europaplatz 3
69115 Heidelberg, Germany

www.ingramcontent.com/pod-product-compliance
Lightning Source LLC
Chambersburg PA
CBHW070959050326
40689CB00014B/3418